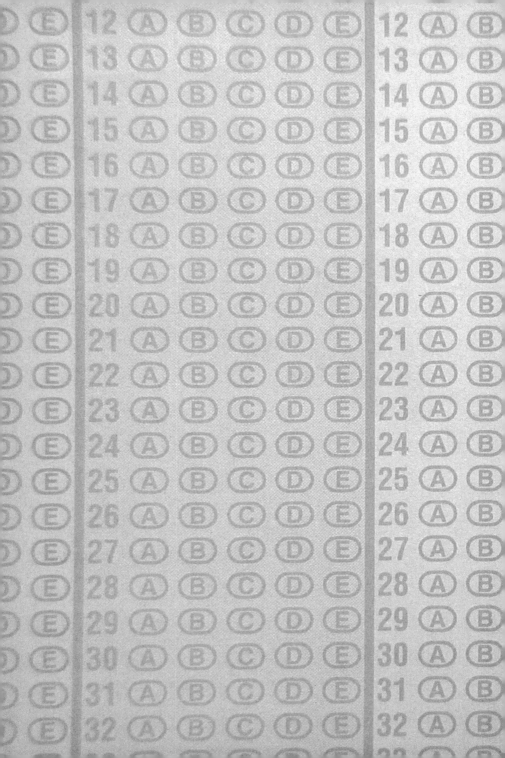

IS IT STILL CHEATING IF I DON'T GET CAUGHT?

by The Ethics Guy®
Bruce Weinstein, Ph.D.

Illustrations by Harriet Russell

Roaring Brook Press
New York

FOR KRISTEN,
MY BRILLIANT AND BEAUTIFUL BRIDE

Text copyright © 2009 by Bruce Weinstein
Illustrations copyright © 2009 by Harriet Russell

Flash Point is an imprint of Roaring Brook Press, a division of Holtzbrinck
Publishing Holdings Limited Partnership
175 Fifth Avenue, New York, New York 10010

Cataloging-in-Publication Data is on file at the Library of Congress.
ISBN-13: 978-1-59643-306-9
ISBN-10: 1-59643-306-X

Roaring Brook Press books are available for special promotions and premiums.
For details contact: Director of Special Markets, Holtzbrinck Publishers.

Cover design by Colleen AF Venable
Cover photo: Keith Brofsky/Getty Images

A portion of "BFF!": Part 2 was adapted from an Ask The Ethics Guy® column
previously published at BusinessWeek.com.

Printed in the United States of America
First Edition April 2009

1 3 5 7 9 10 8 6 4 2

A NOTE TO THE READER:

The questions in this book are composites and are not intended to represent the experiences of a specific person.

Also, nothing in this book is intended to be or constitutes legal, psychological, or therapeutic advice. If you have a question in these areas, please consult the appropriate professional.

CONTENTS

The Basics

Bringing the Principles to Life

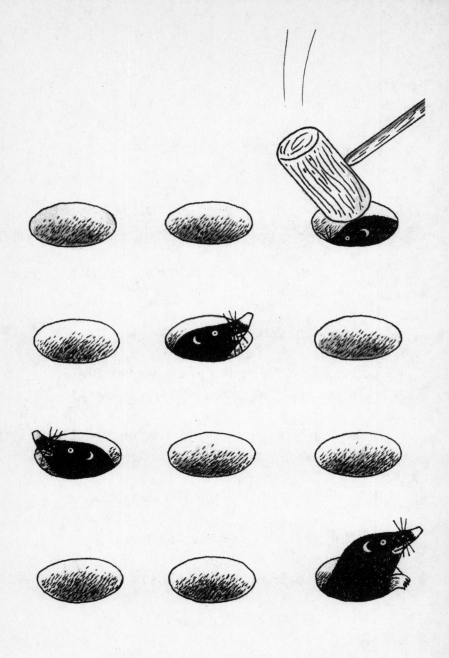

Life Is Like Whac-A-Mole

Have you ever played Whac-A-Mole? The object of the game is simple: Take a rubber mallet and strike a mechanical mole as it pops up through one of many holes on the board. As soon as you hit one mole over the head and it retreats back into its hole, another one pops up. You hit that mole on the head, watch it retreat, and then prepare to smack a third one that will emerge from yet another hole. The object is to hit as many moles as you can in the time allotted. You win if you can hit all the moles before the bell rings. But that doesn't happen very often. After all, it's a carnival game—the odds are stacked against you.

Life can sometimes feel like a carnival game—exhilarating but also unpredictable. You feel that you ought to be able to figure out how to handle whatever life throws at you, but problems seem to pop up at random. The truth is, without a game plan for tackling life's problems, you'll keep whacking away at them with little chance of success.

Wouldn't it be better if life were problem-free?

Not really. A world without any problems would be a dull place to live. After all, overcoming problems can make us better, stronger, and happier. Problems can force us to think of new ways to look at things, bring out qualities that we never knew we had, or prompt us to rethink the way we live our lives.

Some of the toughest problems of all involve doing the right thing. When you ask yourself "What should I do?" you're really asking "What is the *right* thing to do?" Sometimes it's difficult to know what the right thing is, and sometimes, even when you know the right thing, it's hard to find the courage to do it. You may be afraid to talk about the problem with your family or friends, or worry that doing what you believe is right will make you unpopular. You may be concerned that a relationship will be damaged, no matter what you do.

Since life isn't problem-free, the next best thing is to come up with a strategy for tackling dilemmas. It is simply not the case that all of the possible responses to a problem are equally good; there are better and worse ways of playing the game. In other words, just because you *can* do something doesn't mean you *should* do it.

Read on and you'll learn five powerful principles that provide the foundation for doing the right thing anywhere, anytime you're faced with the question "What should I do?" The goal is not for you to become perfect, but to live life to the fullest and continue to be a person you can be proud of.

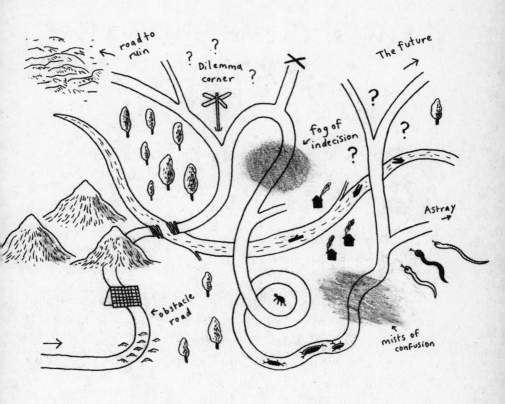

The game of life can be full of pitfalls.

Ethics: The Art of Doing the Right Thing

Ethics is the study and practice of doing the right thing. It is the attempt to answer two basic but fundamental questions in our lives:

1. What should we do?
2. Why should we do it?

The words *ethics* and *morality* are often used as though they represent two different concepts. In fact, the history of the two words is closely intertwined. The Roman scholar and politician Cicero coined the term *moralis*, the root of the word morality, as a translation of the Greek word *ethikos*, from which we get the word *ethics*. Both *ethics* and *morality* refer to doing the right thing, so you can and should use them interchangeably.

The core idea of ethics is simple: In everything we say and do, we ought to think about how our actions might affect other people. But it's a mistake to think that ethics is concerned *only* with how we should treat others. After all, your rights and your well-being are important, too. Ethics is really about finding the right balance between helping others and looking after ourselves. Too much devotion to others can drain you. Too much focus on yourself is, well, selfish. As John Donne, a famous poet, wrote, "No man [or woman] is an island." We need one another not just to survive, but to be the best we can be.

Almost every group you can think of has a code of ethics—a list of rules and principles that serves as a guide-

Self   others

the challenge of ethics

line for proper behavior within the group. Physicians, lawyers, teachers, and journalists are just a few of the professionals who have a code of ethics that tells them what to do, what not to do, and why. In fact, if you take a look at the various codes of ethics out there, you'll see a remarkable similarity among them: "Tell the truth," "Keep your promises," and "Don't reveal secrets" are guidelines common to all professions.

Still, judging from the news and our own experiences, it often seems that the traditional rules and principles of ethics aren't working very well. Too many people seem to live according to the following code:

1. Keep your promises, unless something better comes along.
2. Always tell the truth, unless a lie is more convenient.
3. Do no harm, except when necessary to get what you want.
4. Take the easy way out.
5. Don't make waves.
6. Vent your anger whenever you feel like it.
7. Don't apologize, show compassion, or be forgiving, since these are signs of weakness.
8. Never reveal a secret, unless you have something to gain by doing so.
9. Use your money or connections to get ahead or to get out of punishment.
10. In every situation, ask yourself, "What course of action is most likely to benefit me?"

following the wrong code

Few of us could live very well, or for very long, if everyone followed this code. Think about it: If bullies at school had free rein, you and your friends would live in constant fear of getting hurt. If your parents always lied to you whenever they felt like it, you could never trust them or believe anything they said. If your teachers assigned grades based on what gifts you've given them, rather than on your performance in class, you could be cheated out of the GPA you deserve. In the short run, some of us might benefit by cutting ethical corners, but in the long run, everyone would lose out.

Living ethically isn't just the right thing to do. It's the only way to live well.

MYTHS ABOUT ETHICS

There are a lot of common misconceptions about what it means to be ethical, so before you learn the basic ethical principles, it might help to sweep some of those myths out of the way.

Myth #1: If It's Legal, It's Right, and If It's Illegal, It's Wrong.

In 1955 in Montgomery, Alabama, an African-American woman named Rosa Parks broke the law by refusing to give up her seat on a bus to a white man. She acted illegally but did the right thing, because a good society doesn't make seating assignments on public transportation on the basis of race (or gender or religion or other aspects of a person's makeup or lifestyle). Yes, laws are important in keeping peace and preventing chaos, but they aren't the sole basis for determining what we should or should not do. For any law, we can and should ask "Is it right? Is it fair? Is it just?" Good laws are based on ethics. Bad laws are based on—well, just about anything else. We not only have a right to disobey unjust laws—some would say we have an *obligation* to do so. (Of course, we have to be willing to accept the consequences of disregarding the law, which in Rosa Parks's case meant getting arrested and going to jail.)

Also, consider this: There is no law against breaking promises to your friends, but wouldn't you agree that this isn't the right thing to do? Just because there is no law against doing something doesn't mean that it's okay to go ahead and do it.

Myth #2: If Everyone Is Doing It, It Must Be Right.

Suppose you're at a party one night and you walk into a room in which everyone is using drugs. They're listening to good music, laughing, and having what seems to be a great time. One of the people invites you to join them. If you're tempted to accept the invitation, one of the things that might go through your mind is "Well, how bad could it be if everyone is doing it?" But the fact that an activity is common practice or popular isn't a good reason for doing it. A strong ethical foundation acts like an internal compass that points the way to the right decision, regardless of what others around you may say or do.

Compass with the following labels:
Do it
Do it but resolve never to do it again
Do it but pretend you didn't
Ask your best friend for advice
Don't do it
Get one of your friends to do it
Don't do it but pretend you did
Forget about it and have a cookie instead

Myth #3: If It Feels Right, It Is Right.

"There are no right or wrong answers in ethics," some say. "It's a matter of opinion. If something feels right for you, it *is* right for you." But this can't possibly be true. Imagine how you'd react if you discovered that your boyfriend or girlfriend cheated on you and then said, "It just felt like the thing to do." Or you ended up with a 95 average in math, but your teacher gave you a C and said, "I just felt like giving you a C." In both cases, you have been treated unfairly. In any situation, you can determine the right thing to do only by applying ethical standards that don't vary according to what your feelings are at the moment, or what is convenient, or any of the other excuses people give for doing what they do.

The Five Life Principles

Every day you face difficult decisions, and it's not always easy to know what to do.
Your friends may tell you to do one thing, your parents or teachers tell you to do something else, and there you are, caught in the middle. Everyone means well, but how can you determine the right thing to do?

Obviously, it's impossible to memorize a list of right answers for every possible dilemma that you might encounter. The list of possible questions is infinite, and that means the list of right answers is infinite, too. Since we can't all walk around with the right answers preprogrammed in our heads, the next

Should I...? Shouldn't I...?

best way to prepare for tough decisions is to learn a set of ethical principles.

Principles are general statements that cover a wide range of circumstances. *Ethical principles* are guidelines for doing the right thing. Because these principles are the foundation for how we ought to live our lives, I call them "Life Principles."

They are:
1. Do No Harm.
2. Make Things Better.
3. Respect Others.
4. Be Fair.
5. Be Loving.

Do they look familiar? You probably learned them from your parents and teachers a long time ago. If you practice a religion, you hear about them where you worship. If you belong to a service organization, you go over them a lot. The five Life Principles are simple, and you know them already. Even so, it's easy to forget how important these principles are in everything we do. Every day we're tempted to ignore them and to place value on things that ultimately aren't that important.

Why is it so hard to put the principles into practice? Too often we let fear, anger, or other negative emotions get us off track, and it's sometimes difficult to get back to where we really want to be. For example, how often do you really keep the "do no harm" principle in mind during your daily interactions with people? If a classmate insults you, aren't you tempted to return the insult and tell yourself, "Serves that person right"?

It's understandable that sometimes we let our feelings determine what we do, but that doesn't mean that it's a good idea to let our emotions rule us. Relying instead on your ability to think clearly is a better way to make the best possible decisions, and this is where the Life Principles come into play.

The Life Principles are the Foundation for Your Life

The five Life Principles—avoiding harm, making things better, respecting others, being fair, and being loving— provide the basis for making the right decisions, anytime, anywhere. Just as a house needs a strong physical foundation so that it can be the best possible house, so do you need a strong personal foundation to be the best possible you.

Your foundation comes from the principles that guide the choices you make and how you conduct yourself. You might even say that the kind of person you are is determined by how you choose to act.

Think about the last time you had to solve a tough problem in your life. What got in the way of finding the right solution or acting on that solution? Perhaps it was one or more of the following:

- The problem was so upsetting that it was hard to think straight.
- You were afraid that someone would get angry with you if you did what you thought was right.
- You asked a few people for advice, and you got several different responses.
- What the rules said (or didn't say) was at odds with what you believed was the right thing to do.
- You didn't have all the facts you needed to make a decision.
- You had too much information, and it wasn't clear what was really important and what wasn't.

All of these problems can get in the way of making a good decision and following it through. But they don't have to; understanding the Life Principles can make it possible to work your way through any dilemma. Learn the principles and you will have the tools to make the best possible choices consistently and be the best person you can be.

Life Principle #1: Do No Harm

The most fundamental Life Principle of all is "Do No Harm." That means that, at the very least, we can rightly be expected not to hurt people.

You might be familiar with the "do no harm" principle by its association with the medical profession. Physicians are instructed to "first, do no harm." When we are ill, or when we need a checkup, we go to doctors—and nurses,

Words can be dangerous.

dentists, pharmacists, and other health-care providers—in the hope that they will make us better or help to keep us well, and we rightfully expect that at the very least they will not make us any worse.

But certainly the "do no harm" principle applies to all of us. What kind of society would we have if people had the freedom to hurt others at will and not suffer any consequences for doing so? We would have utter chaos.

While most people know that they shouldn't physically harm people, many people don't realize that emotional harm can be just as damaging. The saying "Sticks and stones may break my bones, but names will never hurt me," may be true for you, but you can't assume that other people feel the same way. Words can hurt, words can wound, and words can leave scars, just as actions can. You can apply the principle of doing no harm simply by choosing not to do or say harmful things.

This principle also applies to how you treat yourself, not just others. It's just as wrong to harm yourself as it is to harm other people. When you don't treat yourself right, you're doing harm to yourself, and you deserve better than that.

In most cases, doing no harm means simply avoiding doing or saying anything that could hurt someone. But sometimes we have to take action and prevent harm to others. For example, if you see that your friend is about to walk into an area where there is broken glass on the ground, you would rightly call out a warning. In doing this, you are preventing your friend from harm that you can see coming but that he or she can't.

taking action to prevent harm

Occasionally, circumstances make it impossible to avoid causing harm, so the right thing to do is to minimize the harm that we regrettably must cause. For example, if you know that it's time to break up with your boyfriend or girlfriend, it would cause unnecessary harm to explain in detail everything you don't like about him or her, including things that the person can't change. The right approach would be to say just enough to make it clear that you don't want to continue the relationship—and leave it at that.

Life Principle #2: Make Things Better

Imagine you're at the end of your life and you're reviewing everything you've ever done. If the most you can say about your relationships with other people is that you never harmed anyone, would you really be able to say that you had lived the best life possible? That you had brought out your full potential as a human being?

It's not enough to avoid harming people. Living ethically also means doing what you can to *help* other people, to bring out the best in others and yourself.

This second Life Principle, "Make Things Better," is where ethics splits off from the law. That is, it's both unethical and unlawful to willfully harm another person. But the law doesn't require us to make things better. We could live our entire lives focusing on only our own needs and desires, and if we do, we haven't broken any law.

Ethics asks more of us than the law does. It invites us—and sometimes requires us—to do more than simply obey the law. Helping other people, enriching the world around us, and being good to yourself are all ways that you can fulfill Life Principle #2.

You will find, also, that you'll be better off when you take Life Principle #2 to heart. That's because making a difference in the lives of others, even in a small way, makes you a more appealing person. Consider this: why do people like you? Is it because you dress nicely, or have a cool haircut, or own the latest electronic gadget? Not at all. The reason people like you has very little to do with your looks or possessions and a lot to do with how you make other people feel in your presence. If people feel good when they're around you, they like you. And contributing something positive to their lives or helping them in some way is a great way to make people feel good. Whether it's assisting a fellow student with her homework, or remembering your mom or dad's birthday, or simply listening to a friend talk about something that upset him, when you enrich the lives of others, you enrich your own life, too.

Life Principle #3: Respect Others

You hear a lot about the word *respect*. You're told to respect authority, respect private property, and respect yourself. But what does it really mean? Fundamentally, it means treating people the way that they want to be treated. It helps, of course, to know in advance how someone wants you to treat him or her. Often, people will tell you if they have specific beliefs or preferences that they want you to respect, whether it's a religious conviction (such as not doing work on their Sabbath), a lifestyle choice (such as being a vegetarian), or simply a matter of personal taste (such as what kinds of toppings they like on their pizza).

But you don't always have to know exactly what a person's preferences are to be able to treat him or her with respect. Most people want others to do the following things on their behalf:

1. Keep Private Things Private

When someone tells you something and says, "Please don't tell anyone else," you show respect for that person by honoring the request. If you don't do well on a test, you expect your teacher not to share that fact with anyone other than your parents. A person has a right to have private things kept private, and that's why others have an obligation to respect that right.

Of course, sometimes you have to disregard a person's wish for you to keep something secret because other considerations rightfully override that wish. If your friend tells you, "I'm going to kill myself, and I don't want you to tell anyone else," you not only have a right to disregard this request, you have an ethical obligation to do so.

Why is that? Because Life Principle #1, "Do No Harm," means, in part, that we ought to prevent harm to others when we can. Although we strive to honor all of the Life Principles, sometimes we must give priority to one over another. In this case, the duty to prevent harm to your friend overrides the duty to keep a secret, because it is more important to save your friend's life than to do what your friend wants. Nevertheless, in most circumstances, it is possible to find a way to honor all of the Life Principles that play a role in a problem.

Don't let the cat out of the bag.

2. Tell the Truth

Another way to show respect for people is by telling them the truth. If your mom asks you how you did on a test and you got a C+, you disrespect her by lying and saying that you got a B.

Telling a lie also shows disrespect for yourself, because lying damages your credibility.

Does this mean that you always have to tell the whole truth and nothing but the truth? If you're testifying in a court

of law, then the answer is yes. *It wasn't me, honest....*
Outside of court, however, the challenge is to be truthful but not to the point that you needlessly hurt someone. If a close friend asks you what you think of her new dress and you think it is unflattering, it would be wrong to say, "That's the ugliest rag I've ever seen in my life, and you're a total fool if you go out in public wearing it." Saying this would almost certainly hurt your friend's feelings and thus violate Life Principle #1.

If you believe your friend really wants to know the truth, it's better to find something you like and mention that (such as, "You look good in bright colors"), along with a truthful statement that isn't likely to be devastating ("But if you really want to know, I don't think horizontal stripes are very flattering to you."). By being truthful but gentle, you're not only treating your friend with respect—you may help your friend make wiser fashion choices the next time she goes shopping, and you avoid making her feel bad.

3. Keep Your Promises

A third way you can demonstrate respect is by keeping the promises you make. You may know someone who makes plans to get together with you and then cancels at the last minute, time and time again. Doesn't that make you feel as though the person doesn't really care about you or respect you? Keeping a promise is sometimes a challenging Life Principle to live up to in an age when people have many different options for how they'll spend their time. But if you think about it, it's one of the best ways to show anyone you care about how much they mean to you. And you shouldn't expect any less from others who say they care about you.

Life Principle #4: Be Fair

What would you say if you and a friend both got every question correct on a multiple-choice test, but your friend got an A and you got a C? I'll bet you'd say, "That's not fair!"

Suppose you're in a spelling bee and you are asked to spell the word *antidisestablishmentarianism*. You don't spell it correctly, so you're disqualified. Then, the next person gets the word *bug*. That wouldn't be fair, would it?

Treating people unfairly isn't rude; it's unethical.

There are at least three ways that we can apply Life Principle #4, Be Fair, in everyday life. All are applications of the idea "Give to others—and yourself—what is due."

1. Distribute scarce resources wisely.

You may think that you're not responsible for distributing any resources, let alone scarce ones, but think again. You manage one of the scarcest resources of all every day: time. Doesn't it seem sometimes that between school, homework, clubs, friends, and chores there aren't enough hours in the day to do what you need to do? Time is your most precious commodity, and if you give all of it to other people and keep none of it for yourself, that's not fair—to you. Managing your time well isn't just a smart thing to do; it's the fair thing to do, too.

2. Punish people appropriately.

Suppose two classmates were caught cheating on a test. As punishment, classmate A has to repeat the entire class next year, but classmate B is given just a warning, because he is a star athlete. That's unfair, because the fact that one person has certain admirable skills or talents shouldn't determine the punishment he or she receives. It is unfair to play favorites. The best rule to follow is Aristotle's: treat like cases alike, and unlike cases unalike.

3. Turn an unjust situation into a just one.

Imagine that you've just been elected president of the school's community service club. In years past, kids joined the club just to go on the annual ski trip, without being required to do what the club is supposed to do: help the community. As president, you rightly see that this situation isn't just, so you make it clear that members of the club will not be invited to go on the trip unless they have participated in its food drives, visits to hospitals, and the like. Ensuring that the benefit of the ski trip is available only to those who have earned it is a marvelous way for you to realize this third aspect of Life Principle #4. (Turning an unjust situation into a just one is also great way to apply Life Principle #2, Make Things Better.)

school

family

friends

me?

Make sure you leave time for yourself.

Life Principle #5: Be Loving

What would life be without love, kindness, or compassion? It would be harsh, empty, and cold. The fifth and final Life Principle directs us to treat others, and ourselves, with care. This is probably the hardest principle to apply on a daily basis. It is also the principle that yields the greatest rewards, both for the people to whom you apply it and to yourself.

Love in the context of Life Principle #5 is more akin to kindness and compassion than to romantic love, and we can and should share this form of love with as many people as possible.

Here are just a few ways that you can apply Life Principle #5 today:

1. Tell someone you care about that he or she means a lot to you and that you are really glad that this person is a part of your life.
2. Ask your mom or dad if there is anything you can do for them without expecting anything in return.
3. When someone helps you in even the smallest way, look him or her in the eye and say a sincere "Thank you."
4. When you're at the cash register at the grocery, convenience, or clothing store, smile at the clerk and ask, "How's it going?" And really mean it.
5. Send an e-card, e-mail, or greeting card to someone special, just to say, "I'm thinking about you."
6. In the next conversation you have, spend more time listening than talking. Really listening. Without judging. Show the other person you are listening by asking questions.
7. Be friendly to the new kid at school.

It takes very little to make a big difference in another person's life. Doing just one of these things will make someone else's day—and yours, too.

Now that we've looked at what the Life Principles are and why they're so important, let's consider how you can apply them in your own life. In the remainder of this book, I'll use a question-and-answer format to describe the kinds of tricky situations you may encounter and how you can use the Life Principles to deal with them successfully.

After each scenario, you'll see a box with a multiple-choice "quiz." You may find that more than one statement captures your own point of view, and in some cases your response may be different from all of the choices listed. Whatever your response happens to be, ask yourself why you believe it's correct. It might be fun to find out how your friends and family members would respond, too, and why.

As you read on, you can and should challenge every single statement in this book. Don't take my word for something just because it's "The Ethics Guy®" saying it. If my analysis of a problem is correct, it is only because of the strength of the argument I'm making and not because I happen to be writing this book. The goal is for you to make these principles your own and to learn how to apply them for yourself. Ethics education—and all education, really—should teach you *how* to think, not *what* to think.

"BFF!" Part I:
Trash Talk,
Promises, and
Cookies That, um,
Don't Taste So Good

Friendships bring us joy—and sometimes challenges, such as how to honor obligations to our friends without sacrificing our own integrity. The Life Principles can offer useful guidance when you're not sure how to respond to the problems that come up with your friends.

SHOULD I TELL MY FRIEND WHAT PEOPLE ARE SAYING ABOUT HER?

Q: I'm best friends with a girl—I'll call her Ashley—who is very popular at school, and as a result, a lot of other girls are jealous of her. Sometimes when I'm at lunch, I'll hear girls say nasty things about her, and they love to spread rumors and gossip. Of course, since I'm Ashley's friend, I never join in, and sometimes I tell them to shut up, but I also wonder if being a good friend means that I should tell Ashley about what people say behind her back.

What Do You Think?

- Ashley should know what people are saying, because I'd want to know what people were saying about me. I would tell Ashley what I've heard.
- The girls are out of line. I'd tell them not to say things about Ashley that they wouldn't say to her face.
- These girls need to be taught a lesson. I'd post stuff about them on my social networking page to get back at them for what they are saying about Ashley. She's my BFF.

A: The unkind things these girls are saying about your friend Ashley are based on jealousy and have nothing to do with Ashley herself. I understand why you feel it might be right to tell Ashley about these attacks. Life Principle #1, "Do No Harm," sometimes means that we have to get involved and prevent harm to others. In this situation, however, the right thing to do is to speak up when you hear these insults—and leave it at that. Here's why.

First, the reason many of us get away with doing or saying things we shouldn't is because no one else tells us to stop. You may have heard the saying, "Silence is consent." Even if you're not actively joining in on the "fun" the other girls are having, remaining silent and not challenging them sends the message that what they're doing is okay with you. But it's not, and that's why you should speak up.

Second, Ashley almost certainly would not want to know that a few people are speaking ill of her, so telling her wouldn't honor your duty to treat her with respect (Life Principle #3). In fact, repeating the slurs would hurt her feelings and thus violate Life Principle #1, "Do No Harm." Of course, if Ashley has told you that she would like a full report whenever anyone talks trash about her, that's one thing, but most people with any degree of self-respect have no interest in hearing the petty things that are said about them.

So how should you handle the situation? It would be both self-defeating and a violation of Life Principle #1 to respond with the same kind of mean remarks you're hearing or to post negative comments on your social networking site. As tempting as it might be to take the low road, you're much better off taking the high road and leading by example. Saying something like, "Ashley is my friend, and I wish you wouldn't say those things about her," is a good way to stick up for your friend and not add to the nastiness. Dealing with the problem this way will show that you're a person of integrity, and you'll have every reason to feel good about that.

Q: Brianna, one of my friends, gave me some cookies she had baked at home. I tasted one, and it was horrible. She asked me, "What do you think?" I didn't want to hurt her feelings, but she asked me for my honest opinion, and I'm supposed to tell the truth, right? So I told her, "Well, um, I have to say they're awful."

Brianna was furious. She said, "Thanks a lot! That's what I get for being nice to you." Now she won't talk to me.

I don't want to lose her as a friend. Should I have just lied to her and told her the cookies were delicious?

What Do You Think?

- Sometimes it's kinder to lie than to tell the truth.
- It's always best to be diplomatic even when someone asks for the truth.
- I'd tell her the plain truth so she can get better at baking.

A: It would be unfortunate if a valued friendship ended over an incident like this. But does saving a friend's feelings justify lying?

Recall that being honest is something that Life Principle #3, Be Respectful, asks—even requires—of us. The critical question here is what Brianna meant when she asked,

choc chip and sardine

"What do you think?" She could have meant, "What do you think of the cookies?" However, she also could have meant, "What do you think of me for bringing you my home-made cookies?" There are good reasons to believe that this second reading of her question is what is really going on here.

Think about it. Most people who ask for your opinion really want to be validated for what they do. They want to feel good for having done something considerate for another person. Can you blame them? While it is noble to do a good deed and not need anyone else to recognize it, most of us want others to appreciate the kind acts we perform, and there's nothing wrong with that. By telling your friend that her cookies tasted awful, you are being truthful, but you're not addressing the larger question being asked.

To honor Life Principle #3, as it applies to this situation, therefore, the truthful answer would have been, "I think it was very thoughtful of you to bring me some of your homemade cookies. Thank you for doing that." Had you said this, your friend would have felt good about herself, as she should, and that probably would have been the end of it.

In the unlikely event that your friend were then to say, "I appreciate that, but tell me what you *really* think," then and only then would it have been fitting to tell her what you thought about her cookies.

Now, does being honest mean being

raisin and spinac

brutally honest? No. Because in addition to Life Principle #3, which directs us to be truthful, we also have to keep in mind Life Principle #1, "Do No Harm." Since one of the ways we can harm people is through the words we choose to use, telling your friend that they were "awful" is truthful but hurtful.

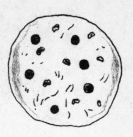

Walnut and salami

If your friend wants to know what it is about them that you didn't like, telling her tactfully could actually be helpful to her the next time she bakes something. Perhaps she over-baked them. Maybe she didn't use enough sugar. Whatever the case may be, being specific about what didn't work for you—without being mean—would both honor your friend-ship and allow you to be true to yourself. Choosing our words carefully in situations like this allows us to apply Life Principle #5, "Be Loving."

You might then wonder, "If it's so important to avoid hurting her feelings, wouldn't it be better just to lie and say I loved the cookies?" No, because then you would be honor-ing Life Principle #1 at the expense of Life Principle #3. Say-ing instead, "Well, I'm afraid I don't really care for them," or words to that effect will be honest but not to the point of making your friend feel bad. We're trying to find a way to be truthful (and thus honor Life Principle #3) and to avoid hurting your friend's feelings (and thus honor Life Principle #1).

By considering the underlying mean-ing of questions such as, "What do you think?" and by taking into account the

Cherry and liver

The chocolate chips taste really good... but maybe you could try leaving out the sardines next time..?

Be diplomatic.

relevant Life Principles, you'll be bringing out the best in yourself and demonstrating that you are a good friend and a kind human being.

WHEN IS IT OKAY TO BREAK A PROMISE?

Q A few weeks ago, I promised my best friend Michael that he could have my MP3 player, since my mom had said I was going to get a new one for my birthday. But last night, my mom sat me down and said she had spoken too soon. When she told my dad what she wanted to do, he said that right now they can't afford it. So now if I give my player to my friend, I won't have one. I don't want to break a promise, but I also can't be without my music—no way! Also, my mom broke her promise to me, so why can't I do the same? My mom isn't a bad person, and neither am I. How should I handle this?

What Do You Think?

- I'd tell Michael that my MP3 player broke and then make sure he never sees me with it.
- I'd "forget" my promise and hope he does, too.
- I'd ask him if he really wants me to go without one now that I'm not going to be getting a new one. If he feels bad for me, maybe he won't care that I promised him mine.
- I'd give him my MP3 player because I said I would and find a way to earn the money for a new one.

A: You're in a tough situation, and it may seem as though you're being punished for being nice. It might also appear to you that you have to choose between being a loyal friend and keeping the music player you love. Let's see, though, if there's a way to do both things. That would be the best solution, wouldn't you agree?

Life Principle #3, "Respect Others," means, in part, that we ought to keep our promises. Does this mean that whenever you make a promise you must keep it, no matter what? With great caution, I say, "Not necessarily." Suppose, for example, you had an open and honest conversation with Michael and explained what had happened. You could say, "I know I promised you my player, but that was when I thought I'd be getting a new one. Since that's not going to happen now, would it be okay if I went ahead and kept it?" A good friend will probably say, "Of course." Being a friend means being flexible and understanding. Yes, you're not keeping your promise, but in this case, it's all right, because the person to whom you made the promise is letting you off the hook.

But what if, for some reason, Michael says, "Hey, you promised, so you still have to give me your MP3 player!" If you go back on your word now, you will be seen as a person who can't be trusted. You say one thing but mean another. Not only are you being disrespectful to your friend (who, granted, isn't being a very good friend by holding you to your promise), you're disrespecting yourself. At the end of the day, all we have is our integrity, and if we start making compromises whenever it's convenient, we may find that we no longer have any integrity left.

Bottom line: Talking honestly with your friend is the best way for you to be true to him and yourself. In the unlikely event that he is not the understanding person you believe him to be, you will be out an MP3 player (and, perhaps, a friend), but you will have kept your word and shown yourself to be an honorable person, which is much more valuable in the long run than any electronic gadget.

Winning On and Off the Field

Sports often bring out our deepest passions. These emotions, and the burning desire to be number one, sometimes give rise to behavior that is questionable, troublesome, or just plain wrong. What do the Life Principles have to say about enhancing performance through steroids, giving everyone a chance to play, and dealing with overzealous parents at ball games?

Q: I play on our school's baseball team, and a lot of the guys take steroids to bulk up. I'm pretty sure the coach knows about it, but he has never said we can't, probably because we are winning in our division this season. I know that this issue is in the news a lot these days, but I really don't see why. I mean, what's the harm? No one I know has developed any of the problems you hear about. I think the whole thing is exaggerated by the media just because it makes a good story. Why do people think it's so wrong?

What Do You Think?

- Taking steroids is wrong. It messes up your body, and that's not worth it to me.
- If you want to be the best, you have to be willing to do whatever it takes.
- If my teammates and our competitors did it and I didn't, I'd have to quit the team.

A: The use of steroids is one of the most important issues in sports today, with implications that go far beyond baseball, football, or weight lifting. It's hard to know whether more athletes are using these drugs than ever before or whether we're simply hearing more about it. Whatever the case may be, the questions raised by performance-enhancing products strike at the heart of what it means to compete in sports.

What harm occurs when athletes use steroids? According to the National Drug Intelligence Center, these drugs can harm the user by altering his or her immune system, making it harder for the body to fight off disease. They weaken bones, making them more vulnerable to damage. They permanently alter the user's voice and even adversely affect the reproductive organs. Other risks include liver and kidney tumors, high blood pressure, severe acne, dramatic mood swings (including manic symptoms that can lead to violence, a condition known as "roid rage"), depression, paranoid jealousy, extreme irritability . . . the list goes on and on. In every respect, the user's long-term health is jeopardized by steroid use.

Since steroids improve strength, it may seem that they are consistent with Life Principle #2, "Make Things Better," but it's a mistake to view them this way. It's *because* steroids make you stronger that they are a problem from an ethical point of view. Steroids cause more harm than good, and not just to the person who uses them—the game being played is damaged.

Steroids harm the user's opponents by making it more difficult for them to win. For example, professional baseball players on steroids can hit the ball harder and increase the likelihood that they will score runs. They harm the sport itself by making it merely a test of artificially created brute strength, rather than a forum for demonstrating how well one can do through a combination of naturally created strength, intelligence, and teamwork. And steroids harm the fans, who pay good money to see a fair-and-square competition but get a bogus, falsified game instead. Steroid use is a blatant violation of Life Principle #1, which directs us to do no harm, as well as Life Principle #3, which tells us to respect others by telling the truth (among other responsibilities).

Life Principle #4, "Be Fair," is also at stake here. Since not everyone who plays sports uses steroids (no matter how common the practice seems to be), those who do use them have strength and endurance that their competitors do not. The advantage was achieved not through hard work and effort (something that comes from within us) but through a pill or injection (something that comes from outside of us). Gaining an advantage simply by ingesting a chemical rather than through sheer will, determination, and effort is a straightforward example of an unfair practice, and this, too, gives us a strong reason for not engaging in it.

A coach who knows about his team's steroid use but looks the other way is not only violating the rules of fair play and the law, he or she is also setting a poor example for the players. A coach should be a role model of good sportsmanship, not someone whose only motto is "Win at all costs."

Q: The coach of our basketball team insists on letting everyone, even the kids who are terrible, play during our games. Granted, they made the team somehow, so the coach must have thought they'd bring something to the game, but maybe they can't take the pressure. When coach puts them in (usually at the end of the game when we're already ahead) instead of those of us who can make the shots, I get really mad, because it's unfair. In my opinion, the coach should either make them work harder during practice or kick them off the team. They need to learn that if they don't make the shots, they don't get court time. I know we'd be winning by bigger margins if some of the other players and I got to play more. The coach says I'm not being fair to kids who aren't as gifted as I am. Who is right—the coach or me?

What Do You Think?

- Whoever makes the team deserves as much court time as everyone else.
- The players who can't perform at the same level as everyone else should be benched or cut.
- Everyone knows the best players should get the most court time. That's the only way to have a winning season.

A: Both you and your coach invoke the ethical principle of fairness, or what we're calling Life Principle #4. For you, being fair in sports means "only the most skillful get to play," while for your coach it means "everyone gets to play."

Let's assume for a moment that your interpretation of the principle is correct. How is someone supposed to develop their skills if they are not allowed to play in an actual game? After all, it's one thing to play when the stakes are low (for example, at the gym in between games). It's quite another thing to play when you're in competition with another team and the clock is running. Higher stakes mean more adrenalin for both the players and the fans, and when there is more on the line, we are forced to reach deep within ourselves and rise to the challenge of the moment. There is simply no alternative to the demands of playing during a real game.

However, there will always be players who just can't become as good as others, no matter how hard they practice. Does fairness require that these kids, too, get a chance to play? Absolutely.

Your coach recognizes that the students who aren't so good could jeopardize the team's chance of victory, so it is appropriate that these players are allowed to play when this isn't likely to happen. After all, the point of any game is to win. That said, winning isn't the only thing that sports should be about. They should also foster team building, camaraderie, and fun. If fairness is about giving others their due, then it seems downright harsh to prevent the lesser-skilled kids from playing at all. It's one thing to prevent them from getting in the way of the team's success. It's quite another to stop them from enjoying the thrill of actually playing the game. It is not only possible but preferable to find a way both to give the most skilled players a shot at winning (by playing early in the game) and the not-so-adept kids a chance to have fun on the court (or playing field, or whatever the sport in question happens to be).

One more thing: you never know when one of those kids who can't seem to throw a ball will prove everybody wrong and score.

Everyone should get a chance.

Q: Something has been bothering me for a long time. I play on a softball team, and the parents who come to the games sometimes get into shouting matches with the coaches, the umpire, and even each other. I've heard parents make threats, and once a fistfight even broke out in the stands between two fathers. Some of the parents even yell at their own kids and say horrible stuff like, "If you don't get a hit, you're walking home." It's embarrassing to see adults (including, I hate to say, my own parents) take the competition so seriously. Don't get me wrong; I want to win as much as anybody. It's just that I don't see the point in getting so riled up about a game. I have two questions, really. Isn't it hypocritical for adults, who are always telling kids what's right and wrong, to act worse than their kids do? Also, what should I do the next time this happens?

What Do You Think?

• Sports naturally bring out the aggressive side in everyone. I can see why parents get upset at games.
• Parents shouldn't be yelling at their kids or anyone else during a game. They should take the high road and set a good example.
• Kids should call their parents out if they can't control themselves at a game. Parents are too involved in their kids' lives.

A: I'd like to think that parents are the last people who would behave improperly, but this is sadly not always the case.

Unfortunately, parents aren't immune to having the same behavioral problems that they criticize (and sometimes punish) young people for. The conduct of these adults is not only immature—it's wrong. Such harsh, disrespectful, and unfair behavior violates all five of the Life Principles.

In sports, it is just as important to lose with dignity as it is to win graciously. Anyone can throw a temper tantrum when an umpire or referee makes a call we don't like, or gloat and preen when we defeat our opponent. It takes a mature person to resist the impulse to be childish or let anger get out of hand. Anger isn't just a psychological issue; it's an ethical one, too, because expressing our anger can cause others to fear for their safety.

It is thus a violation of Life Principle #1, "Do No Harm," and Life Principle #2, "Make Things Better," to mismanage our anger.

Parents who engage in such wrongful conduct are showing great disrespect to their children and to the other participants, so they are violating Life Principle #3, "Respect Others."

Uncivil, threatening, or violent behavior at a sporting event is also a

Grrr.... come on, Son!

violation of Life Principle #4, "Be Fair," since it disrupts the game and makes it harder for the participants to play well. This shows that fairness in sports applies not just to the participants but to the fans as well.

Parents make mistakes just like everybody else. This is an explanation, not an excuse, for the unruly conduct you describe. In answer to your first question, yes, it *is* hypocritical for them not to practice what they preach, even though we can understand why parents slip up from time to time. In answer to your second question, Life Principle #5 calls upon us to be loving and compassionate, even—or especially—when others are not acting this way. You can and should condemn the conduct while also recognizing that adults are sometimes all too human.

The bottom line is that it is inexcusable for anyone to engage in such unsportsmanlike behavior as getting into a fight, threatening another person, or just expressing anger inappropriately. One of the reasons that people get away with this kind of foolishness is that onlookers don't take a stand against it. The players should make it clear that everyone in the stands is expected to treat each other respectfully, and anyone who acts in an uncivil manner will be required to leave—including parents. I'll bet your policy will be respected.

Meetups, Hookups, and Breakups

Can you put the five Life Principles aside when you go out on a date? Why would you want to? After all, following the principles can help win your date over. Who wouldn't want to spend their time with someone who's kind, respectful, and loving? And when it comes to ending a relationship, remember that people beyond your ex will know how you behaved. Acting ethically can help smooth over the rough edges when a relationship ends. The principles can help you navigate the tricky waters of looking for love or dealing with a relationship that has run its course.

Do I HAVE TO USE A REAL PICTURE IN MY ONLINE PROFILE?

Q: Last week I created a profile on one of the popular social networking websites. I had a dilemma, though, because if I had posted my real picture, no one would contact me. Most people judge you on the basis of how you look, and I'm short and overweight, so I decided to put a picture of someone I found on the Internet. (I don't know the person, but it was a good picture of someone about my age.) I figure I'll make a lot of friends and that if people ever want to meet me, I'll send them my real photo. If they're really my friends, they will understand why I put someone else's picture in my profile. If they're not true friends, then it won't matter if they get mad. My best friend thinks I should put my *real* picture up. What do you think?

What Do You Think?

- It's better to post a good picture than a bad one even if it's not your own. Who will ever know?
- It seems wrong, but I'm not sure why. I guess I just wouldn't want to fake out other people, even if I don't know them.
- I would never post someone else's picture and try to pass it off as mine.

pretending to be
someone you're not

There are several problems with posting someone else's picture in your online profile.

Life Principle #3 tells us that we ought to treat others with respect, and one of the ways we show respect for people is by being honest. Putting another person's picture in place of yours is simply dishonest. You're leading people to believe that you are someone you aren't. Using another person's photo without that person's consent violates Life Principle #3 in another way, too: It is deeply disrespectful to the person whose image you are stealing. You would most likely feel wronged if someone used your photo without your knowledge or permission. Why, then, wouldn't you expect someone else to feel the same way?

What might not be immediately obvious, though, is that you're also being disrespectful to yourself in several ways. First, you believe that no one would contact you if you posted your real picture. But your online profile isn't just about how you look; it's about what kind of person you are. Think about the things you love to do that a lot of other people also enjoy doing. You didn't mention your hobbies, but whatever they happen to be—playing chess, listening to music, going to the movies, playing video games—you can bet that a lot of other people out there share your passion, and they will seek you out and become your friend no matter what you look like. Yes, there are some shallow people who value looks above all else, but they're not the kind of people you want in your inner circle anyway. When you post someone else's picture in your place, you're not just lying to others, you're lying to yourself. You're essentially saying, "I'm not good enough to be liked the way I am." That simply isn't true, and the fact that you have friends right now who accept you as you are is proof of this.

Now let's consider the role that Life Principle #5, "Be Loving," plays in this situation. The idea that we should be kind, loving, and compassionate applies not just to how we treat others, but also to how we treat ourselves. Being so hard on yourself because of the way you look is unkind—to you.

Taking Life Principle #5 to heart means changing the things about yourself that will benefit you (such as developing better eating habits and exercising regularly) and accepting—and even embracing—the things about yourself you can't change (such as your height).

Finally, Life Principle #2 invites us to make things better, and Life Principle #4 tells us to turn an unjust situation into a just one (or, in other words, to right a wrong). The way you can put these principles into action now is to remove the picture you put up and replace it with your own.

Is it okay to break up by e-mail?

Q A guy I've been dating for several months just did something horrible, and I want to see what you think of it. We were in love, or at least I thought so. He goes to a different school, and we met at a football game. We clicked instantly, and pretty soon we were doing everything together. It got to the point where he was all I was thinking about night and day, and he told me he felt the same way about me. But then a few days ago he sent me an e-mail.

Here's what it said:

I don't think we should go out anymore. I'm sorry. It's all just been going too fast for me. I'm not ready to be tied down to one girl. I was going to call you, but I thought this would be easier on you. Maybe we can hook up down the road some time, but for now, I need to take some time off. I hope you don't hate me. Again, I'm really sorry. I'll always love you.

Can you believe that? I've been crying nonstop since I got it. I'm angry at him, angry at myself, and mostly I feel like an idiot for falling for this guy. Don't you think it's wrong to break up with a person by e-mail? I feel he owed me more than that. My sister says I should just forget about him, but it's not that easy.

What Do You Think?

- Forget about this guy and find another one, fast, to take his place. That'll show him!
- Learn to be a better judge of character next time around.
- Spending all day and night thinking only about one person is a mistake.

A: In this situation, the boyfriend violated Life Principle #3, "Respect Others," in the way he chose to handle the breakup. He also showed little compassion for you or your feelings, so he was reckless with Life Principle #5, "Be Loving," as well. Although he claimed he used e-mail because "it would be easier on you," it's more likely that he ended the relationship this way because it was easier on him. It's never easy to break up with someone (unless they're being abusive, and sometimes even then it's hard to let go). When it is time to end a relationship, we ought to do so as respectfully and compassionately as possible. And that means that, although it might be difficult, you should make an effort to talk in person, or at the very least, over the phone. Breaking up by e-mail is wrong in this situation because it is disrespectful, unkind, and selfish.

But it's also possible to get deeply emotionally involved too quickly. Even after a few months of nonstop dating, it's hard to know who the other person really is. People aren't always who they appear to be.

As we've seen throughout this book, the five Life Principles apply to how we treat ourselves, not just how we

treat other people. Launching into an intense relationship with someone you don't know very well makes you emotionally vulnerable, and that's not a very kind way to treat yourself. It's not wrong to think about your own needs—such as the need to be secure—a little bit more the next time you feel you click with someone. I know it's hard to show restraint when it all feels so right. The challenge is to find a balance between being selfless and selfish. Going too far in one direction benefits no one in the long run.

And one more thing. If he contacts you "down the road some time" and wants to get together, consider this: the best predictor of future behavior is past behavior. He has already shown himself to be a selfish person. Yes, people can and do change, but only if they recognize that there's a problem and are willing to do some hard work to correct it. You would need strong evidence for it to be worthwhile to trust this person again.

WHEN IS AN OLDER GUY TOO OLD?

My favorite camp counselor asked me out on a date. I've had a crush on him all summer, and I would love to go, but I know my parents wouldn't allow it. My counselor told me he'd meet me somewhere that my parents would never find out about. I don't want to lie, but what other choice do I have? I'm a teenager, and even though he's out of college already, he's not married, and I don't see anything wrong with it. I always see adults dating people who are many years younger than they are, and no one makes a big deal about that. It's not like he's a teacher at my school; that would be gross. Besides, if my parents really knew him the way I do, they would see what a great person he is. Don't you think that in some circumstances, it's okay not to tell your parents certain things? What they won't know won't hurt them.

What Do You Think?

- Who people date is their business.
- I'd keep the counselor as a friend until I got older and then see what develops.
- A counselor who would ask out a camper isn't someone you should get involved with. Dump him or her.

A: It might not seem obvious why dating a camp counselor is similar to, say, dating a teacher (which is a violation of a teacher's ethical responsibilities and could be against the law). But a camp counselor who is out of college and who dates a camper—even one who is an older teen—may cause harm to that camper in ways that may be felt for years afterward.

In a way, a counselor at camp is like a teacher. He or she has the responsibility to look after your interests first and foremost and is thus more like a caregiver than a peer. Because of the large age difference, a romantic relationship with a counselor would almost certainly put you under pressure to get involved sexually faster than you might want. If this counselor is truly looking out for your welfare, he or she would know to keep your relationship friendly but not romantic.

The boundaries of being a good counselor stop at getting romantic with campers, and rightly so. By asking you out on a date and encouraging you to lie to your mom and dad, your counselor is showing great disrespect to you and betraying the trust your parents have placed in him. Such a serious violation of Life Principle #3 should be a red flag in any relationship.

Also, whenever there is an imbalance of power or authority between two people, there is the potential for abuse and the violation of Life Principle #1, "Do No Harm"—even if both people in question are adults. This is why it is unethical for physicians to date their patients, or attorneys to date their clients, or teachers to date their students. If someone is significantly more powerful or influential than you are, it may be difficult for you to resist doing what that other person wants. You might reasonably fear, for example, that your doctor won't give you the proper medical attention if you decline to get romantically involved with him, and this fear may become a reality if you do turn him down or end the relationship on your terms. Whether it feels this way or not, there is indeed an imbalance of power between you and your camp counselor, so it is wrong for your counselor to see you as a potential girlfriend.

Please consider this, too: If your camp counselor were to become sexually involved with you, he would probably be committing statutory rape. There are good reasons why the

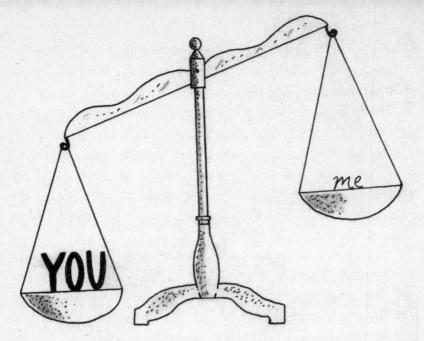

In love, an uneven balance of power spells trouble.

law prohibits an adult from getting romantically involved with a minor, even if the minor consents to the relationship. It is an exploitation of a young person's vulnerability and may cause substantial harm to him or her.

In answer to your question, there are a few things it may be okay not to tell your parents about (such as what you're writing in your diary or journal). But dating your camp counselor isn't one of those things. A crush can be understandably overpowering, and everything else in comparison can seem insignificant. In this case, however, the crush is best left unexplored. You would do well to tell your parents about all of this, because your camp counselor should not be allowed to do this kind of work any longer.

Should I Do Anything for Love?

Q: My boyfriend and I have been together for six months, and we're really in love. We do everything together: go to movies, do our homework (even though he's a grade ahead of me), play tennis and racquetball, and even do some volunteer work downtown. I've had other boyfriends, but he's the first I consider to be a true soul mate, and I know he feels the same way.

Lately he has been saying that he feels it's time to take our relationship "to the next level" and have sex. Part of me would really like to do this, but another part of me feels I'm not ready for it yet. I know it sounds weird to say that because it seems like everyone is having sex, but I guess I just want to make sure that the time is right, and right now I don't feel it is.

When we have disagreements, which isn't all that often, we're usually able to resolve them before they get out of hand. On this issue, though, he doesn't want to take "no" for an answer. Don't get me wrong; he would never force himself on me. He's not that kind of guy at all. But he'll say things like, "If you really loved me, you would show me."

I'm not a prude, and I really do love him, but I don't feel I have to prove my love for him by having sex. I feel he should respect my decision and leave it at that. I'm worried, though, that if I take this position for too long, he'll want to go out with other girls (some of whom would have no problem going along with him). What's the right thing to do?

What Do You Think?

- He's right. If you love someone, that means having sex.
- Feeling pressured into doing something you're not sure about is wrong. A boyfriend or girlfriend should understand.
- Get ready to get dumped.

A: Pressuring someone to have sex is a major violation of Life Principle #3, "Respect Others." After all, the way we show respect for others is by honoring their wishes and values. By trying to persuade you to sleep with him, your boyfriend is showing great disrespect for you, and that's just plain wrong.

Another sign that he is failing to respect you is his statement, "If you really loved me, you would show me." You don't have to show your love by doing something you don't want to do, especially when that something is as special, intimate, and risky as sex is. This would be the case no matter how old you are, but the fact that you are both

We respect each other

under eighteen makes it especially so. The best way to show true love is by respecting what our partners want, not by imposing what we want on them. You could just as easily say to him, "If you really loved me, you would respect my decision to wait!"

You should never have to worry that being yourself and expressing what you want will bring about an end to the relationship. If your taking a stand leads this guy to drop you for someone else, he wasn't the right one for you in the first place.

I'm not saying that all is lost with this person, but his behavior and choice of words present a major red flag. Since mutual respect is the core of any meaningful relationship, you should tell him that you expect him to honor your wish not to have sex, and that if he can't, you'll be the one to walk away. How he responds will reveal his true character.

We work as a team

Self-Defense:
Bullies, Pushers,
and Critics

What should you do when someone pressures you to take drugs? What are your options when you're being bullied? How should you respond to criticism, which can sometimes hurt more than a physical attack? We'll look at all three of these issues now.

Q: There is a guy at school named Matt who loves to pick on smaller kids. I'm one of them. Sometimes he asks for money, sometimes he calls us names, and sometimes he shoves us into a wall or the lockers when the halls are crowded. He likes to threaten us with other violence, although I've never actually seen him hit anyone. If people are going to hurt me, I think I have a right to hurt them back, or at least defend myself somehow. I've seen ads for things like pepper spray and stun guns, and I'd like to get one of these devices so that I don't have to be afraid of going to school. I think that's better than telling the principal; the whole school would find out if I did that and make my life miserable. Don't I have a right not to be picked on? What's wrong with wanting to protect myself?

What Do You Think?

- Anyone who bullies other kids gets what they deserve if the people who are being picked on fight back. It's okay to use any means necessary to defend yourself from being attacked.
- It would be better to ignore this guy than to fight him. Bullies always come back for more if they know they can get to you.
- You should tell the principal, the dean of discipline, or anyone else in charge that this guy is bullying you. You don't stand a chance without adults on your side.

A: You absolutely have a right not to be picked on, and Matt has no right to bully anyone. His behavior violates of all five of the Life Principles. But there are several good reasons why arming yourself with pepper spray or a stun gun isn't the best way to respond to the situation.

First, in some states it is illegal to use these weapons, no matter how old you are. But even if you would be breaking no law in giving Matt a dose of his own medicine, so to speak, a canister of pepper spray is more likely to be used against you than by you. After all, by your own admission, Matt is bigger than you, and it wouldn't be that hard for him to wrestle the can away from you and make you the victim. You can take a look on the Internet and find out exactly what kind of damage pepper spray can cause: temporary blindness, painful burning that lasts a long time, and a lot more. Your understandable effort to protect yourself can wind up making you worse off than you were before.

Your teachers and principal have a responsibility to make sure that all students are protected from harm. They want to know about troublemakers in their midst, and sometimes the only way they can learn who these troublemakers are is if students like you tell them what's going on.

The kids you fear will give you a hard time for telling one of your teachers about Matt may be kids who Matt or some other bully will pick on one day. Since Life Principle #4, "Be Fair," means that we should give to others their due, letting a responsible adult know about a bully like Matt is the right

SPEAK UP!

thing to do. The kids you protect may not thank you for it, but you will be doing them a huge favor by speaking out.

It may seem strange to bring Life Principle #5, "Be Loving," into this discussion, but it is fitting to do so. Did you ever wonder why a kid like Matt feels he has to use violence to solve his problems? Matt may be singling out kids who are smaller and weaker than he is because someone close to him (say, his father or an older brother) is doing exactly the same thing to him. This doesn't excuse what he is doing, but by trying to understand the cause of his behavior, you may be able to see the situation as it really is and then find out the right solution to the problem.

Look at Matt not with contempt and hatred, which is all too easy to do, but as someone who may not be as fortunate as you and whom you may be able to help. At the very least, taking the high road will bring out the best in yourself and, perhaps someday, in a young man who needs to find better ways of responding to his own problems.

Having said all of this, learning how to defend yourself against bullies is consistent with all of the Life Principles and something we all need to learn. Take a karate class. Lift weights. Regard yourself as someone who deserves respect. The way you carry yourself can send a clear signal that you

Help!

are not someone others will be able to take advantage of. There are ways of disabling an attacker that will get you out of danger and make them think twice about messing around with you. Having to use force against an opponent is not something you ought to look forward to doing, or be happy about when you have to do it, but if someone refuses to back off and the choice comes down to you or that other person, you come first.

THE PUSHERS

Q There's a kid I see from time to time at some of the parties I go to. He doesn't go to my school, but some of the guys in my class know him from the soccer team they're on. He asks me sometimes if I want to buy some pot from him. I've turned him down before, but he'll usually say something like, "What's wrong? Chicken?" A few of the other kids are getting on my case about trying it, too. They ask me, "How do you know you won't like it if you've never tried it?"

My mother and father would be *so* angry if I took drugs, even just to try them once. But I don't like to be made fun of, either. Also, when you think about it, how do you know what something is like until you try it? We're talking about pot, not something serious like heroin or crystal meth. What's wrong with trying a joint to see what's it like?

What Do You Think?

- I'd buy the joint and just pretend to smoke it so the other kids would stop hassling me.
- I'd stop hanging around with this crowd.
- If I keep getting pressured to try it, I probably will at some point.

A: In the United States, it is illegal to buy and sell marijuana for recreational use. Period. Whether this law is just or not is something we could debate, but such an argument isn't relevant here, unless you're willing to risk going to jail and paying a fine just to smoke some pot. I'll assume, therefore, that of all the laws you might want to challenge on moral grounds, the prohibition against buying a dime bag isn't one of them.

I will also put aside a discussion of the physiological and psychological ways in which smoking pot is harmful, because I'm sure you're already familiar with them.

What this problem is really about is not the relative benefits and dangers of buying and smoking pot, but whether it's okay to give in to peer pressure. Consider this: If someone wanted to sell you something that he or she honestly believed was good for you, would that person have to resort to calling you "chicken" to make the sale? Anyone selling drugs doesn't care about you. They just want you to become a repeat customer, and their main concern is themselves. Their taunts aren't worth taking seriously, as unpleasant as those taunts may be.

Now let's look at the claim that for you to be in the know about something, you have to experience it yourself. On the face of it, this seems to make sense. After all, it's one thing to read about, say, what it's like to travel around the country, but you don't really know how much fun this can be until you actually do it. On closer inspection, however, the claim misses the real point. It may be necessary to experience something to know what it is like, but it is not necessary for you to experience something in order to make a moral judgment about it. Do you have to be a victim of torture to know

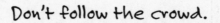

Don't follow the crowd.

that torture is wrong? Do you have to steal something to be able to say, "It's not right to be a thief"? You don't have to engage in the illegal activity of smoking pot to see what the consequences of that choice would be and to conclude that this is something a reasonable person would want to avoid.

Peer pressure is powerful. Everyone wants to be liked, and it's unpleasant to feel as though you're the odd one out. But if you consider that the call to do no harm (Life Principle #1) and respect others (Life Principle #3) applies not just to how we treat others, but also to how we regard ourselves, then the right response to this dilemma is clear: Turn down the "opportunity" to buy pot from this guy and anyone else who offers it, ignore the insults the kids toss at you for not being "cool" enough to take drugs, and be true to yourself and your parents. Mom and Dad are the people who truly care about you.

THE CRITICS

Q It seems like everybody is always on my case. My teachers are always telling me to do this, do that, don't do this, don't do that. My band director is impossible to please, and no matter how hard I practice, he finds something wrong with my playing. My parents are constantly griping about what I need to do or what I should have done better.

Sometimes I feel like nothing I do is ever good enough for anyone. Don't you think it's unfair to criticize someone all the time? I'm sick of it.

What Do You Think?

- It's okay to sit your parents down and say, "Get off my case. It's my life and I know what I need to do."
- Quit band. Who needs to be hassled over something that's supposed to be fun?
- Ask the adults who seem so critical to tell you exactly how you can do a better job and then to cut you some slack as you try to do your best.

A: I wish I could say that being criticized is something you'll experience only when you're young, but I'm afraid it's something you'll face throughout your life. Is criticism necessarily a bad thing? Let's take a closer look at this.

No one wants to admit that they're flawed or less than perfect. We like to think highly of ourselves, and criticism seems to contradict this. However, since we all have room for improvement, criticism can be helpful, not hurtful. When criticism is expressed appropriately, we should feel better, not worse, about ourselves because we now have an opportunity to grow. Even if you tend to be hard on yourself, sometimes other people can see problems that you can't (or won't) see in yourself.

Still, there are good and bad forms of criticism. The good

kind focuses on your actions, which is helpful because you can correct the problem. The bad kind includes personal attacks ("You're an idiot"), broad statements ("You always do the wrong thing"), or vulgar language (you can supply your own examples here). The purpose of criticism should be to help someone improve what they're doing or who they are, not to bring someone down and instill guilt or frustration.

Offering good criticism is one of the best ways to apply Life Principle #2, "Make Things Better," and taking care not to be too harsh honors both Life Principle #1, "Do No Harm," and Life Principle #5, "Be Loving." Since respectful criticism is a powerful way of fulfilling Life Principle #3, "Respect Others" (part of which involves telling the truth), all five Life Principles are at stake in this issue.

Of course, even the good kind of criticism can sting. It's neither possible nor desirable to completely eliminate all of the unpleasant feelings you may experience in life. When you're not measuring up to the best you

CRITIC'S RULER

The Best
Outstanding
Fantastic
Very good
Good
Fair
Okay
Acceptable
Not quite good enough
Poor
Bad
Very bad
Terrible
The worst

can be, it's entirely appropriate to feel angry, hurt, or disappointed when someone suggests that you're not doing a good job.

I realize that it can seem as though the criticism is constant, but take a step back and look at the situation as objectively as you can. As hard as everyone is on you, are there also times when you are recognized for the good things that you do? Taking those times into account may make the criticism easier to bear.

If parents and teachers are being disrespectful in their criticism, then you can and should say something, like "I don't deserve to be talked to that way. If you treat me with respect, I'll be happy to listen to what you have to say." You have a right to stand up for yourself, as long as you do it respectfully.

You should ignore criticism that is insulting, nasty, or personal and realize that it says more about your critic than it does about you. Insults violate Life Principle #1, "Do No Harm," since we can harm people not just by what we do but also by what we say. This sort of criticism also violates Life Principle #5, the duty to treat others with kindness and compassion.

For those times when your critic has a point, as difficult as it might be to accept, I suggest doing this: Listen carefully to the criticism. Don't resist it and don't defend yourself. If you're truly receptive to what your critic has to say, you just may find their criticism useful. If you act on the criticism rather than rejecting it, you may very well end up better off than you were before.

Getting Tangled in the World Wide Web

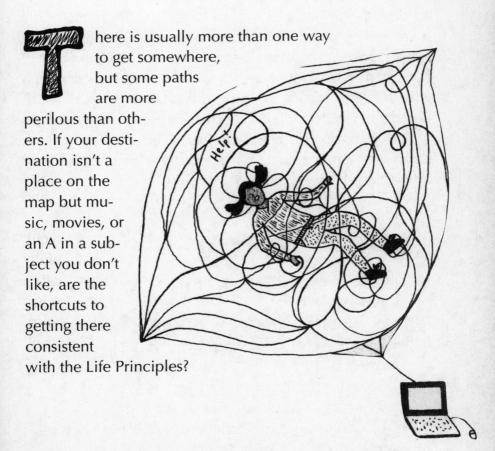

There is usually more than one way to get somewhere, but some paths are more perilous than others. If your destination isn't a place on the map but music, movies, or an A in a subject you don't like, are the shortcuts to getting there consistent with the Life Principles?

Q: One of my teachers assigned a novel for us to read that is really long and looks boring. There is no way I am going to read a book like this. For one thing, I'm on the debate team, and we have a lot of tournaments out of town on the weekends, which means I don't have much time to do all of my homework. For another thing, it's hard for me to concentrate on something I'm not interested in. I end up reading the same passages over and over.

Still, it's very important to me to get good grades. There's a website a lot of kids use that sells essays on just about every book ever written. These essays are really expensive, and I don't have a lot of spending money, but in the long run it's worth the sacrifice to avoid getting a bad grade or an incomplete, which could bring down my grade point average.

Isn't it wrong for companies to take advantage of students and charge such high prices for essays that they know kids will need to buy?

What Do You Think?

- It's wrong for companies to take advantage of kids this way.
- It's not wrong. This is a business like any other. If you don't want to pay the price, you can do the work instead.
- It's wrong for companies to sell these essays, and it's wrong for kids to buy them.
- It's not wrong because they're available on the Internet, so it's obviously legal.

A: Some assignments are hard, some are frustrating, and some are, yes, just plain boring. Nevertheless, the ethical question you're facing is not "Should companies charge a lot of money for essays that students want to buy?," but rather "Is it right to buy essays in the first place?"

The answer is easy: No, it's not right to buy essays, whether online, from a friend of yours, or by any other means. For any reason.

Here's why.

Your teacher assigns book reports to help you develop your reading and writing skills. You may feel as though you've mastered those skills, but even professional writers continue to work on them. Reading books for yourself gives you knowledge you wouldn't have had otherwise, and writing essays gives you critical practice that eventually adds up to solid skills. Failing to do your homework causes harm to you by diminishing your educational experience and thus violates Life Principle #1, "Do No Harm."

Life Principle #4 calls upon us to treat one another fairly. When you buy an essay, you're being unfair to your fellow students (at least the ones who are writing their own papers). You're being unfair to your teacher, who trusts that the work you turn in will be your own. And you're being unfair to yourself, because you're pretending to be someone you're not—the author of the paper to which you attached your name.

Also, recall that Life Principle #3 says that we ought to treat one another with respect, and one way to show respect for people is by telling them the truth. Turning in an essay that someone else wrote is a lie, and it's disrespectful of your teacher's right to be told the truth.

Lying is a bad habit to get into, because telling one lie and getting away with it makes it easier to tell another, and then another. Suppose, for example, that after you turn in your counterfeit essay (which, after all, is what it is), your teacher becomes suspicious about whether you actually wrote such incredible work on your own. You'll then have to come up with some believable story about how you managed to write such an amazing essay, and you'll have to fake being offended that your teacher would dare to question your integrity. Pretty soon, your credibility will be damaged, and you may even begin believing your own lies.

It's not easy to keep a ruse going for very long. A little detail will give you away, or other people will. You got this essay on the Internet, so isn't it possible that another student in your class will turn in the very same one? Telling the truth isn't just the right thing to do—it also makes life a lot easier.

There is another issue worth addressing here. When you refer to the website for buying someone else's work as one that "a lot of kids use," are you implying that it's okay to do something if other people are doing it, too? That just isn't right. Kids around the world bully other kids, but the fact that such violence is common or widespread doesn't make it right.

When we apply these principles—ethical principles that have stood the test of time—to the issue of buying essays for school, it becomes impossible to justify such a practice.

The bottom line is this: If this is the book you're assigned to read, then this is what you have to tackle—honestly. You'll feel better about yourself in the long run if you write the essay yourself and get the grade that reflects the real you—rather than someone far away who made some money at the expense of your integrity.

One more thing: How do you know you won't like the book? You may just find it's not as bad as you think—and you could even end up enjoying it.

WHAT'S SO WRONG WITH BUYING PIRATED DVDs?

Q This guy downtown sells DVDs of movies that just came out in theaters. Sometimes he gets movies that haven't even opened yet. He sells them for $5 each, which is a really good deal, since even a child's ticket at the theater costs more than that where I live. My parents say it's wrong to make them and wrong to buy them, but I don't see why. We don't have a lot of money, and these DVDs are affordable. It's too expensive to go to the movies these days. Why should people who aren't rich be deprived of being able to see the latest movies like everybody else?

What Do You Think?

- If you really want to see a movie that badly, you should rent it when it comes out on DVD.
- It's okay to buy a pirated DVD, if you have the chance.
- Why spend even $5 for something that may turn out to be a rip-off?

A: Yes, going to the movies is expensive. The question is this: Does being short of money justify buying pirated DVDs (that is, DVDs that are illegally made and distributed)? Before we consider what the Life Principles have to say about the matter, let's look at how pirated DVDs are made and why this raises ethical concerns.

The process starts when someone goes into a movie theater with a small camcorder. He or she records the movie secretly and then makes a DVD from this amateur recording. Artwork made by the movie studio is reproduced and incorporated into the packaging for the DVD, which is copied and sold directly to the public. Let's be clear about one thing: Making these kinds of DVDs is both illegal and a violation of the policy of movie theaters. Many movie theaters now advise patrons that anyone found recording the movie will not only be thrown out of the theater, but will also be subject to civil and criminal penalties; in other

words, violators may have to pay a lot of money in fines and perhaps even go to jail. The same is true for the unauthorized replication of studio artwork used in the packaging of the DVDs.

Making pirated DVDs is a form of theft, since it involves taking someone else's property without their knowledge or consent. The people who make movies work hard to create a film you will like, or at least be willing to pay to see in the best possible circumstance (i.e., a movie theater with a big screen and accurate sound reproduction). They invest a lot of resources, not the least of which is "sweat equity," or their hard labor, in making something for your entertainment. Buying a pirated DVD robs the filmmakers, the graphic artists, and everyone else connected to the movie of

the chance to be paid back for their work. Making, selling, and buying pirated DVDs are all violations of Life Principle #4, which calls upon us to treat one another fairly and to give to others their due. After all, when someone does work, he or she is entitled to be compensated for that work.

Tough economic times can make it difficult for a lot of folks to go out for an evening's entertainment. Does that mean that you can leave a restaurant without paying for your meal, or swipe some gadget from an electronics store, just because you're short on cash? Of course not. By the same token, it's wrong to buy a pirated DVD because that, too, is theft, even if it may feel different from the other two examples.

Who cares if it's illegal to download music?

Q: I don't understand why a lot of people make such a fuss about downloading music for free from the Internet. Why would anyone want to pay for something you can get for nothing? To me, it's not stealing at all. Stealing is when you walk into a grocery store and take a can of soda without paying for it. That's wrong, because you're physically taking something that doesn't belong to you, and the store had to buy that can of soda somewhere. But when you download a song, someone has already bought the CD or music file somewhere, and that person is just sharing it with others. No one is losing any money. To me, the sites with free digital songs on them are like radio stations, even if technically speaking they're illegal. Actually, they're better than radio stations, because you get to choose which songs you want to hear—and you get to keep the music, too.

A lot of the free music out there comes from bands that are already rich anyway. They don't need any more money. What's the big deal with downloading songs for free?

What Do You Think?

- If music is out there for downloading, why not?
- I wouldn't do it, but I don't blame others for doing it.
- Some of my friends do it, but I think it's wrong.

A: The big deal is that downloading songs (or movies) without paying for them is indeed stealing, and for this reason it's wrong.

Why does stealing have to be limited to "physically taking something that doesn't belong to you?" Hackers who drain a person's bank account online are stealing that person's money, but they're not physically walking into the bank to do it. So the fact that you're not physically taking the song does not mean that the practice isn't stealing.

It's also not true that the practice is justifiable because "no one is losing any money." By taking a band's music without paying the band for it, that group is being deprived of the money they would have gotten had you paid for it. Also, some of the money that we pay when we buy a song goes to the writer and the publisher of the music that the artist is playing, as well as the company that produces the song. This includes the producer, engineer, and the executives at the label that record the song and make it available for people to hear.

It really all comes down to this: When person A does work for person B, person A deserves to be paid for that work, unless person A has said upfront that they're donating their services to person B. Life Principle #4 calls upon us to treat one another fairly—that is, to give to others their due. A band may be making music not because it's work to them but because they want to express themselves creatively, but very few bands want to give their music away. Even if they did, the people who record their music and make it available to the world certainly want to be paid, and they have a right to be.

It's true that sometimes a band will offer a free download of their music online for promotional purposes. They hope that if you like one song, you'll buy the rest of their music. Some bands will even offer an entire album for free. They may want to create loyal fans, or to reward their current ones, by offering something for nothing. But that doesn't mean all of that band's music is up for grabs.

Your statement that "a lot of the free music out there comes from bands that are already rich" doesn't hold up, either. The truth is that most

artists, whether their art is music, film, painting, writing, dancing, or acting, are not even close to being wealthy. They often have second (or third) jobs to make it possible for them to make music, direct a film, write a novel, or act in a play. For them, the few dollars that you're not paying them for the song they've written, performed, and recorded is significant, especially when you multiply that amount by the number of other people who are taking their music without paying for it.

However, whether an artist makes $2 or $2 million dollars from their art is irrelevant to the matter at hand. Stealing is stealing, even if the person you're stealing from won't be financially ruined from the theft.

Beyond this, it is illegal to download music for free without the consent of the artist, and that provides a very strong reason for not doing it. Of course, just because something is illegal does not necessarily mean that it's wrong. But if you consider the laws against downloading music for free to be unjust, and you believe you're entitled to engage in this practice, you have to be willing to pay the price for your beliefs. This might mean being liable to record companies for hundreds of thousands of dollars should you be caught and sued for violating the law. Are you willing to pay such a price? Is such a penalty even worth it?

Using the term "sharing" to refer to the practice of illegally downloading songs from the Internet implies that the person whose work is being passed around has given his or her consent, and that isn't true here. Paying for the songs you download is the fair thing to do, and the right way to say "thanks" to the people who make the music you enjoy.

"Gotcha!": Spoiling, Cheating, and Taking Advantage of Another's Mistake

Is it wrong to tell the end of a movie to someone who hasn't had a chance to see the movie yet? Are there circumstances in which copying answers on a test could be okay? Do you deserve to keep a high grade if the teacher made a mistake? The Life Principles can illuminate the answers.

The main character's best friend ends up in the hospital

Q: There's a guy in my grade—I'll call him John—who thinks it's really funny to tell people how a movie ends before they find out on their own. John usually sees a movie the weekend it opens, and then on Monday morning, he'll come to school and tell everybody the ending, whether we want him to or not. When I tell him I don't appreciate this, he'll say something like, "I'm not telling you anything you wouldn't have found out sooner or later. Movie critics give the ending away, so why shouldn't I? Lighten up. It's just a movie."

Who's in the wrong—John or me?

What Do You Think?

- I would walk away from John when I see him coming.
- Whether it's John or people posting spoilers on the Internet, who cares if you know the ending of a movie?
- I would keep trying to get John to change. Someone has to!

A: There are good surprises and bad surprises. Finding out for yourself what happens at the end of a story is a good surprise. Having that ending revealed to you without your consent is a bad surprise. Spoiling isn't innocent fun, and you're not hypersensitive for getting upset when this happens to you.

Spoilers like John aren't bad people, but what they're doing is wrong. If it makes you feel any better, you're not the only person who has had someone ruin the ending of a story for him or her. Right before the final book in the Harry Potter series was published, a few people like John went to great lengths to reveal the ending of the story. They went to chat rooms, online bulletin boards, and fan websites to give away major plot developments before the fans could find out for themselves. One person even posted the ending in the readers' comments section of an online column I wrote about the ethics of—get this—spoiling the ending of the last Harry Potter book.

Shame on the spoilers! It's not only rude to reveal secrets. It's unethical. Here's why.

First, fans of a book, TV show, or movie invest a lot of time, and a lot of themselves, in a story. Spoilers violate Life Principle #1, "Do No Harm," by revealing the ending of a story before the fans are able to discover it themselves. Spoilers may not consider what they're doing to be

she marries the handsome prince

harmful, but those on the receiving end of their actions certainly do.

Second, a story doesn't appear out of thin air. It is created by someone. That person, the artist, would be understandably upset to learn that a person like John has revealed the surprise of the story on which he or she has worked long and hard. Spoilers harm not only the fans of an artist's work, but the artist as well.

In other words, "Do No Harm" applies not just to how we should treat the readers of a book. It also applies to how we should regard the artist who wrote the book and to the culture that makes such art possible in the first place.

Another ethical consideration here is Life Principle #3, "Respect Others." Ruining the ending of a story is disrespectful, since it violates what most people want, namely to experience the pleasures of that story on their own. John seems to care more about showing that he's the first to see a movie than respecting those who can't get there on opening weekend. That doesn't make him a bad person—just a self-centered one.

Finally, spoiling violates Life Principle #4, "Be Fair," which tells us to give others their due. Spoiling the ending of a book or movie is unfair to people, since it deprives them of the right to enjoy a story in the same way the spoiler did: without anyone ruining it for them.

Read me and find out for yourself...

How should you deal with spoilers? It would be easy to respond with insults or threats, but doing so would violate your responsibility to avoid causing harm and to treat others with respect. Just because the spoilers don't take Life Principles seriously doesn't mean that you shouldn't, either. Better to appeal to the spoiler's better nature ("I know you're a good person at heart, so please don't ruin the surprise for me"), or simply to avoid that person to the extent you can. Parents of a spoiler, however, should look into an appropriate punishment. It's only fair!

WHY IS IT MY PROBLEM IF SOMEONE ELSE CHEATED?

Q This morning when I was taking a test, I noticed a girl named Hannah copying answers off of the person next to her. She looked around and saw that I had seen her—apparently no one else had (including the teacher, who was reading a book). After class, she came up to me and told me not to tell anyone what she had done. She said it was the first time she'd ever cheated and the only reason she did it was because she was going through a difficult time at home. She said her parents were getting a divorce and she hasn't been able to concentrate on her homework. She promised she would never do it again, and said that I should do the right thing and keep it to myself.

The thing is, we have an honor code at school, and we're supposed to report violations of the code to our teachers. But I'm not a rat. Besides, if she is telling the truth about her parents, I can see (sort of) why she did what she did.

What should I do?

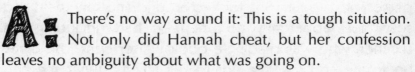

What Do You Think?

- This girl is obviously going through a tough time. Give her a break.
- Even if you see someone else cheating, it's not your business to say anything.
- Cheating is wrong, and anyone who cheats should be punished. I had to study and take what I got on the test. Why can't she?

A: There's no way around it: This is a tough situation. Not only did Hannah cheat, but her confession leaves no ambiguity about what was going on.

There is also the matter of a violation of the school's honor code. Presumably that code does not say "Students may not cheat, unless they are going through a difficult time at home, or have just broken up with someone, or simply didn't feel like studying." More likely, it says that if you present someone else's work as your own, you are cheating, and you will be punished accordingly. It doesn't matter why the student was copying someone else's answers. Cheating is cheating, whatever the motivation happens to be.

Not all schools have an honor code, and it's easy to think that if there isn't one, you have even more reason not to "squeal." Without knowing clearly what is expected of you when you witness wrongdoing in school, it might be tempting (even if it's not justified) to forget about the whole incident and go on with your life. In this situation, however, it is clear what the school requires of you, as difficult as it may be to put that into practice.

Life Principle #4, "Be Fair," is one of the ethical considerations that plays a role in this dilemma. Cheating is one of the most flagrant violations of this principle. Suppose that the person you saw cheating winds up with an A as a result of copying the answers from someone who achieved that grade through hard work. Two people are now being treated unfairly: the person Hannah copied from, whose grade now means less, and Hannah herself, who is posing as someone she isn't. Actually, everyone in the class who did honest work, whether or not it resulted in an A, is being treated unfairly by the cheater. They would be right to say, "I studied for this exam and got an honest grade, but the cheater got the best grade possible without doing any work for it. That's not fair!"

Let's now consider what might happen if you go along with what Hannah has asked of you. She may very well cheat again. One of the reasons many people continue to cheat is because they haven't been held accountable for their actions, so if you keep this incident to yourself, you're

I'd rather not be a . . .

essentially telling Hannah that she can do something wrong without having to worry about getting punished.

Of course, telling the teacher what you witnessed isn't a guarantee that Hannah won't repeat the offense. For that behavior to stop, the school has to be willing to punish her and make it clear that further misconduct will not be tolerated. She also has to make a commitment not to cheat again. Teachers, parents, and schools can do their best to prevent students from taking the easy way out, but ultimately it is up to students themselves to do the right thing.

The reluctance to be a "rat" is understandable, but consider this: What might happen to you if your teacher finds out that you knew about the cheating incident but did nothing about it, even though the honor code required you to take action? The teacher may sympathize with your situation and would certainly be more upset by what the cheater did herself. Nevertheless, your teacher may feel quite disappointed that you didn't come forward, as difficult as that would have been for you to do. You may also have to face a reprimand from the school for not following the honor code.

The bottom line is that keeping quiet just isn't the right thing to do for a variety of reasons. I'm afraid that you have no alternative but to inform your teacher about what you saw. No one likes having to do such a thing, but you have nothing to be ashamed about. After all, you haven't done anything wrong.

When we consider how the school should respond to Hannah's conduct, Life Principle #4, with its call to punish wrongdoers in the appropriate way, is obviously important. But Life Principle #5, "Be Loving," is also at stake here. If Hannah is telling the truth and she really is experiencing a turbulent home life, then she would benefit from counseling, which the school can provide. Yes, she should be punished for what she did, but a compassionate response would include not only punishment, but also help.

WHAT'S THE PROBLEM WITH WALKING INTO A MOVIE THEATER WITHOUT PAYING?

My friends and I found a cool way to see two or three movies for the price of one. The movie theater we usually go to has 12 screens. After our movie lets out, we call a few friends, get some popcorn and candy, and then walk right into the second movie we want to watch. If it's Friday or Saturday night, we can even see a third movie this way. My friend Ali saw me doing this and said that it was wrong. I told Ali that it's not like we're sneaking in—there usually isn't any usher around, so we're not doing it behind anyone's back. And it isn't stealing, since the movie would be playing whether or not we're there. Who's the victim?

What Do You Think?

- Cool idea. I'll have to try it some weekend.
- Ali is right. You pay for one show and that's all you're entitled to watch.
- It's not right, but if the theater doesn't send anyone to check tickets, it's really their problem, not mine.

A: Stealing means "taking something without paying for it." In this situation, you are in fact taking something—namely, the experience of watching and enjoying a movie—without paying for it, so what you're doing is indeed stealing. The fact that you don't have anything tangible to show for it, such as an article of clothing or DVD, isn't relevant.

Life Principle #4 says that we ought to treat people fairly by giving to others their due. By getting something for nothing, you're not being fair to the theater owner, who has to pay the movie studios for the privilege (not the right) to show their films. You're also not being fair to the people who made the movie you're watching for free. This includes the producer, the director, the actors, and all of the technicians who make the film possible. They, too, deserve to be paid for their labor. Thus, the answer to "Who's the victim?," is "Everyone who made it possible for you to watch the movie in the first place."

The practice of auditorium hopping might not land you

in jail, but you could be banished from the movie theater for a long time. There is an even bigger price you pay by taking something for nothing: you chip away at your own integrity. The five Life Principles, including "Be Fair," have to do not only with how we treat other people, but also with how we treat ourselves. Resisting the temptation to get something for nothing is a good way for you to be fair to yourself as well as to others.

It is said that our true character is revealed by how we act when no one is looking. This situation is a great test of who you really are, and who you want to be.

Is an accidental A good luck or ill-gotten gains?

I'm not very good at math, so I was really surprised to see that I got an A on my final exam. I knew I didn't do that well on it, so when I looked it over, I saw that my teacher had added up my score incorrectly. (Kind of ironic, huh?) Anyway, I will now get a B in the class, instead of the C that I would have gotten. Needless to say, a B would look a lot better on my transcript, so of course I don't want to tell the teacher that she gave me the wrong grade. Also, I feel that since my teacher made a mistake, I shouldn't be penalized for it. I don't want to tell anyone what happened, because I'm afraid the word will get around and the teacher will find out. All I want is to get a good grade. Is that so wrong?

What Do You Think?

- What a stroke of luck! Take it and keep quiet.
- Keep the A, but be prepared in case the teacher realizes her mistake and changes your grade back.
- Tell the teacher and get it over with. Who needs the guilt?

A: Of course it's not wrong to want to get a good grade. What's wrong is getting it through someone else's error. I suspect that you know it's wrong, too. Otherwise, why be afraid of the word getting out? Knowing that it's not right to claim a grade you didn't earn means that you have a conscience, and that's a good thing indeed.

Consider Life Principle #4, which tells us that we ought to treat one another fairly. How would you feel if your teacher decided to assign grades not on the basis of how well students did on exams, but on what color their hair happened to be? Imagine her saying, "Students with blond hair get an A, black hair a B, red hair a C, and brown hair a D." If you're not blond already, you could dye your hair blond, or you could say, "That's not fair! What does that have to do with how well I do in math?" You want a good grade in class, as does everybody else, but what would an A mean if you didn't earn it? "Give to others their due" is what it means to be fair, and if you earned a C in the class, then that is what is due.

Suppose that your teacher had made a mistake in the opposite direction: She incorrectly added up your score and got a D instead of an A. Wouldn't you speak up in that case? Of course you would, and you would be right to do so. By the same token, it would be just as wrong to keep the A to yourself. You're not being penalized for pointing out her error; you're correcting an injustice (which is another way that we apply Life Principle #4 in everyday life). In other words, speaking up rather than keeping the mistake to yourself shows the world that you are a fair person. Quite frankly, it's also admirable, since a lot of people in your position would take the easy way out and keep silent about the error.

It may not feel like it, but keeping a grade you didn't earn is a form of theft. As we saw with the auditorium-hopping situation, taking something that doesn't belong to you doesn't have to involve something tangible like a book or candy bar. For example, imagine that you and the class are out on a field trip and you stop at a restaurant for lunch. With so many kids to serve, the waiter accidentally forgets

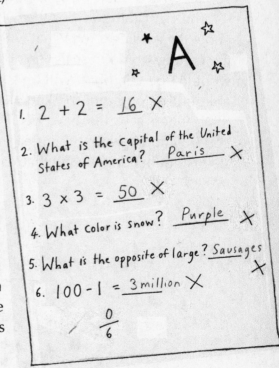

to charge you for the piece of chocolate cake you ordered for dessert. Would it be right to pay the check without mentioning the error? Of course not. You'd be getting something for nothing, and that's wrong. (Consider this as well: The waiter might have to pay for your dessert out of his own pocket.) From an ethical point of view, remaining silent about the A you received as a result of your teacher's mistake is no different than walking out of a restaurant without letting the waiter know that he forgot to charge you for dessert.

Life Principle #3, "Respect Others," is also at stake in this situation, since one of the ways we honor this principle is by being honest. At some level of your being, wouldn't you feel like a fraud if you kept quiet about the mistake?

The right thing to do, then, is to let the teacher know about the grading error. What will your reward be for having the courage to do this? It won't be keeping the A, since that wouldn't be fair, but it will be something much more valuable in the long run: the knowledge that you did the right thing when it would have been a lot easier not to do so. You'll wind up with a C instead of a B, it's true, but you'll sleep a lot better knowing that you are a person of integrity.

"BFF!" Part 2:
Messing Up, Fessing Up, and Forgiving Your Friends

Friendships are great when they're going well. The real test of a friendship, however, is what happens when things don't go so well. When, if ever, should you apologize to a friend if you've messed up? Must you always accept a friend's apology when he or she messes up with you? Is it possible to apologize too much?

Friendships need TLC, too.

Q: Andrew has been my best friend for a couple of years now, but we recently had a fight, and I don't know what to do. We have different religions, and usually this doesn't come between us, but it did the other day. Here's what happened: We were arguing about which comic book hero could beat all of the other ones put together. I told him who I thought would win, based on the characteristics of each superhero. Andrew thought a different character would win, but out of nowhere, he starts quoting religious texts to support his position. I laughed and told him it was stupid to bring religion into it. He got really mad at me and said that if I felt that way about it, we couldn't be friends anymore. Huh? I told him that I didn't say his religion was stupid; he was being stupid for talking about religion here in the first place. But now he won't speak to me, and I don't know what to do. I'd hate to lose him as a friend, but if he's that sensitive, maybe he's not worth keeping as a friend after all. What should I do?

What Do You Think?

- Andrew needs to lighten up. If he doesn't, he is the one who is not being a good friend.
- Andrew is right to feel insulted, and he is owed a sincere apology.
- Andrew shouldn't be so upset, but his friend should be more careful about what he says about Andrew's religion.

A: Suppose that Andrew said something that really bothered you, and when you called him on it, he just laughed. Wouldn't the fact that Andrew refused to take your feelings seriously be worse than whatever it was that ticked you off to begin with? If so, that would be understandable.

When we take another person's feelings for granted, we're disrespecting that person, and thus violating Life Principle #3, "Respect Others." Respecting a person means honoring his or her beliefs, particularly when those beliefs are important to that person. Even friends—especially friends—should respect one another's feelings, and when a friend feels insulted by something you've done, it behooves you to take that insult to heart and to apologize.

WHEN YOU OWE AN APOLOGY:

- Admit your mistake quickly and take personal responsibility for it.

- Apologize first to the person you have wronged. That is the person who matters most.

- Speak from the heart. An insincere apology is as bad as no apology at all.

- Realize that *sorry* is just a word. For that word to be meaningful, you must do your best to avoid repeating the mistake. This means coming up with a strategy and sticking to it.

- Understand that a meaningful apology is a sign of integrity, not weakness. Anyone can blame others, or deny that he or she did anything wrong, or lie about what really happened. Only a strong, self-possessed person can own up to his or her mistakes, and only such a person commands true respect.

It isn't easy to apologize, but you'll feel better about yourself if you do, and you'll be salvaging a friendship that, by all appearances, is well worth keeping. Mainly, though, you'll be showing your respect for another human being, and that's all to the good.

SHE SAID SHE'S SORRY. SHOULD I FORGIVE HER?

Q One of my friends recently did something that really upset me. She apologized later, but I don't know if I should accept her apology. This is the story: Some kids were making fun of the fact that I just got braces. They taunted me for days, even though I told them it wasn't funny and that I wanted them to stop. One of the people in this group was my friend, Madison. At least I thought she was my friend. I couldn't understand why she kept calling me names, since I let her know over and over that I didn't appreciate it. She called me last night and said she was sorry. Her excuse was that she just wanted to go along with everybody else and didn't want the other kids to think she was taking sides against them. I can see how I should accept someone's apology if they made a mistake, but Madison insulted me on purpose, and she kept doing it even though I asked her to stop.

The thing that hurts the most is not all the insults but the fact that I thought Madison was my friend. Should I accept her apology or tell her that I don't want to be friends with her any longer?

What Do You Think?

• Madison is not a friend. A friend would never insult you on purpose.

• Madison is probably insecure and doesn't really know how to be a good friend. At least she was honest, though.

• You should find a way to do the same type of thing to Madison so she'll know how it feels to be on the receiving end. Then say, "Now we're even." It will feel better, even though you'll probably never be friends with her again.

A: It's one thing to tease someone in a good-natured way for a little while, but to continue taunting someone after they've made it clear they don't appreciate it is wrong, because it's a violation of Life Principle #1, "Do No Harm"; Life Principle #3, "Respect Others"; and Life Principle #5, "Be Loving."

To Madison's credit, she had the courage to call and apologize. A lot of people in her situation would wait until they happened to see you at school, making it easier on themselves (if they even bothered to apologize at all).

However, *I'm sorry* is just a few words strung together. For these words to matter, they have to be backed up by action. Thus, you have every right to expect Madison not to engage in such mean-spirited "games" again. You would also be justified in questioning why Madison would feel it necessary to join in with the other kids in the first place. Being someone's friend means sticking up for them when they need support, as you did then. It would have been bad enough if Madison had just stood there while the other kids made fun of you, but to join in is inexcusable. Yes, we all want everyone to like us, but if we have to make a choice, we ought to support our friends, even if this means that not everyone will be on our side.

Consider how it will affect you if you tell her that you

don't accept her apology. Not only would you be ending the friendship, but you risk holding a grudge against her. What does it do to you to hold a grudge against someone? It may have little or no effect on the person you don't forgive, since he or she will probably move on and forget about the whole thing. It will, however, make you bitter and resentful, and that isn't a good way to be. Life Principle #5 calls upon us to treat one another—and ourselves—in a kind and compassionate way, and holding a grudge simply isn't a very kind way to treat ourselves. Forgiveness shows compassion both for the person who has wronged us and for ourselves, too, since it takes us beyond the grudge we may be holding.

Life Principle #4 tells us that we should be fair in how we treat people, and if someone offers us an apology in good faith, fairness (along with compassion) requires that we take the apology to heart and forgive the offense. We are, however, entitled to expect that the other person will do their best not to repeat the mistake or give in to the less-than-noble impulses. Thus, when you get back to Madison, it would be gracious to accept her apology—and fair to let her know that you expect a friend to stick up for you, not contribute to your misery. Only time will tell if Madison makes good on her apology and shows herself to be a true friend.

WHEN SOMEONE OWES YOU AN APOLOGY

If someone has done something wrong and apologizes to you, accept the apology graciously. However:

- You are also justified in expecting the person to avoid repeating the behavior that required an apology in the first place.

- Depending on the situation, you might need to make clear to the other person what the consequences will be if he or she makes the mistake again.

- If someone has apologized but continues making the same mistake over and over, you may have to say, perhaps regrettably, "I really can't give you another chance," no matter how much that person continues to apologize.

IS IT POSSIBLE TO APOLOGIZE TOO MUCH?

Q My girlfriend and I have an ongoing argument about apologizing. She says that whenever I do something wrong, I should say, "I'm sorry." To me, though, apologizing is a sign of weakness. For this reason, I don't like to say "I'm sorry," especially if the situation isn't a big deal. My girlfriend, on the other hand, apologizes constantly. If you bump into her by accident, she'll say, "I'm

sorry." If she needs directions to a store, she'll stop someone and say, "I'm sorry, but can you tell me how to get to
this place?" When she makes a mistake, even a small one,
she apologizes over and over. I think this makes her look
like she doesn't have any self-confidence. She says that it's
just common courtesy to say you're sorry when you incon-
venience someone or mess up in some way. Who's right?

What Do You Think?

• It's good to apologize, but don't overdo it.
• Common mistakes don't call for an apology. It's
best to let some things ride.
• Apologizing is the right thing to do in any circumstance.

A: It's just as wrong to apologize too often as it is to not
apologize enough. Here's why.

Life Principle #3 affirms our responsibility to treat one another with respect. Offering a sincere apology when we make
a mistake is one of the ways we show respect. Recall also that
one way we apply Life Principle #4, "Be Fair," in everyday life
is by correcting injustices. Making a mistake that hurts another
person is a form of injustice, so apologizing for that mistake—
and doing our best to avoid repeating the mistake—is a powerful way of making Life Principle #4 come alive.

Of course, just saying "I'm sorry" doesn't really do much more than inform the person you've wronged that you regret what you did. For an apology to be meaningful, it has to be backed up with a strategy for avoiding making the mistake again. That isn't a guarantee that the mistake will never happen again, but it does show the other person that you're apologizing in good faith, and it gives you a plan for doing a better job next time.

You say that "apologizing is a sign of weakness." A lot of people share your point of view. However, if you look closely at what's going on when someone apologizes, I think you'll see that it's actually a sign of strength. It takes courage to admit that you've done something wrong. Refusing to apologize when you have clearly done the wrong thing, rather than owning up to your mistake, is actually the weak thing to do.

By the same token, it is quite possible to apologize too much. If you apologize for things that clearly aren't your fault, the words *I'm sorry* lose their meaning. Now, your girlfriend may be using these words not to admit guilt or blame but to express her feelings of regret that something unfortunate has happened, such as someone bumping into her. In that case, "I'm sorry" stands not for "I'm sorry I made a mistake," but rather, "I'm sorry that we're both sprawled out on the floor after you tripped running down the hall." It is kind, I suppose, for her to express her condolences, but it's really the other person who should be saying, "I'm sorry." Even when your girlfriend is the one who has made a mistake, though, saying you're sorry too much is just as much of a problem as not saying it enough.

two situations of differing seriousness

Minimum Wage, Minimum Work?

There is no getting around it: Work is hard. It might not seem obvious at first, but many of the challenges about work have to do with ethics. Let's take a look.

Is it okay to come to work late if I'm really tired?

Q I just got my first job: delivering newspapers in my neighborhood after school. I thought it would be a good way to get some extra spending money, but it's not as easy as I thought. For one thing, when school lets out, I'm pretty tired, so I usually take a nap when I get home. Since the job started, though, I haven't been able to do this. I have to roll up the papers that arrive in a bundle at our house as soon as I get home and then ride my bike around and deliver them for an hour.

The worst part about the job is that my boss gets on my case if I'm even thirty minutes late getting the papers delivered. He says that customers call him and complain if they don't have their newspapers when they get home from work. I think it's unfair of customers and my boss to expect me to do my job before I even get a chance to relax a little. My boss says that he is going to fire me if I can't get my job done on time. You say that one of the Life Principles is "Be Fair." Well, doesn't that mean that people should be fair to me, too?

What Do You Think?

- If you can't do a job the way you're expected to, you should be fired.
- It's not okay to be late every day, but on occasion the boss should cut a kid some slack.
- The boss should understand that kids' lives are as stressful as adults' today. I'm sure adults want to take a nap and relax when they come home from work. It's no different for a kid.

A: Yes, people should be fair to you, but are you being fair to your customers and your employer by being late more than once or twice?

Life Principle #3, "Respect Others," entails keeping our promises to one another. When you accept any job, you and the company essentially make a promise to each other. You promise your employer to do the job asked of you, which is usually during a specific period of time. Your employer promises to pay you. If your boss called you one day and said, "I'm sorry, but we can't pay you any longer, though we still expect you to deliver our papers," wouldn't you say that they couldn't rightly expect you to work for free? If they broke their promise, then the arrangement you've made together would no longer be valid, and you would no longer have an obligation to work for them.

The same goes in the other direction, too. When you decide to take a nap and show up late for your paper route, you're breaking a promise to your employer. If you do it often enough, your employer can legitimately say, "You've broken your promise to us, so we're letting you go."

Life Principle #4, "Be Fair," calls upon us to give to others their due. If your employer wants you to take on 50 new customers, you would be entitled to be paid accordingly for this extra work. It would be unfair for your employer to expect you to do this out of the goodness of your heart. By the same token, however, you owe it to your customers to deliver their newspapers in a timely fashion, and you owe it to your employer to do your best to meet the needs of these customers. It's one thing to miss a day because you're sick and aren't able

to do your paper route that day (though you would still have an obligation to let your employer know you can't work that day). It's another thing to choose to do something else that will make you late for work.

It's understandable that a nap after an exhausting day of school would be refreshing. You owe it to yourself to be the best you can be, which means being awake and alert when you have to be and taking some time off when possible. The goal for all of us is to honor our responsibilities to ourselves and to others. The situation you describe seems to suggest that you have a conflict between what you owe yourself (i.e., some time to relax after a hard day) and what you owe to others (i.e., delivering papers in the late afternoon). There may be a way, however, to do both things.

Perhaps you can do the paper route only on the weekends, when you could get the job done early in the morning and then relax for the rest of the day. If you're able to go to bed earlier, you won't be so tired after school and will be able to do the paper route on time. Or perhaps it would be better to leave this job and get one that isn't so hard to manage.

The habits you develop in your first job will carry over into jobs you have after you finish school. Yes, it's important to treat yourself well by getting enough rest. It's also important to honor the commitment you make to your employer and your customers. If you're able to do both, you will show yourself to be a person of integrity, and you will be a valued member of any team fortunate enough to hire you.

WHAT'S WRONG WITH MAKING A FEW PHONE CALLS WHILE I'M BABYSITTING?

Q The other night I went over to my friend Stacy's house to keep her company while she babysat her little brother, Jake, and her parents went out for dinner. We let Jake play video games while we got online and IM'd some friends. Then my boyfriend called me on my cell phone, so I talked with him while Stacy stayed on the computer.

Well, her parents came home earlier than they said they would, and they got really mad at Stacy—and me! They said it was irresponsible of her to be distracted while Jake was in her care and that I should have been looking after Jake if Stacy wasn't doing it. For one thing, Jake was never in any danger. For another thing, I don't see why Stacy and I had to spend every waking minute looking after her brother. Don't we have a right to have a little fun, too?

What Do You Think?

- Babysitting someone's little brother or sister doesn't count as a real job, so you shouldn't have to abide by these restrictions.
- With two people babysitting, one should always be available while the other is busy. Then trade off so you can each have some fun.
- Babysitting is a responsibility, and that means paying attention to the child you're watching, not just enjoying yourself.

A: The word babysitter is misleading. You're not sitting around with a baby, which suggests that you're being passive. A more accurate word is *caretaker*. This suggests, quite rightly, that you're actively involved in ensuring that the child is safe from harm and occupied in some meaningful way. This is why it is irresponsible for babysitters and parents alike to feel that they're doing their job simply by putting a child in front of a TV or video game for a few hours. To take care of someone is to give more than just your time to another person. It is to give something of yourself to him or her. It is also one of the best ways to apply Life Principle #5, "Be Loving," in everyday life.

When Stacy agreed to look after her brother while her parents went out, she was making a promise to them. Therefore, Life Principle #3, "Respect Others," is at stake here, too, because keeping a promise is an important way that we show respect to someone. There is a lot more going on in this simple scenario than one might think.

There's nothing wrong with having a little fun. As Life Principle #4 suggests, being fair means that we have to be fair to ourselves as well as to others. However, there is a time for looking after one's own needs, and there is a time to stay focused on meeting the needs of others. If Stacy wants to IM her friends and you want to talk with your boyfriend on the phone, you both have every right to do so, but not when you are being charged with the most serious of all responsibilities: caring for someone who cannot care for him- or herself.

Stacy's parents were justified in reacting the way they did.

OKAY, IT'S GROSS, BUT DO I HAVE TO REPORT IT?

Q ▨ I work at a local fast-food restaurant. Yesterday, my manager did something really gross. I saw her leave the bathroom without washing her hands. I didn't say anything, because I thought she would get mad and possibly fire me, and I need the job to earn money for college. We were super-busy yesterday, so probably she was just in a rush and forgot. Don't you think that sometimes it's okay not to speak up so that you can protect yourself?

What Do You Think?

- Don't jeopardize your job and the money you need for college by saying something to the boss.
- If this was the only time this ever happened, it was okay not to speak up, but if it happens again, I would say something.
- It's wrong for a boss to violate the health code, so she should be reported right away.

A: Yes, sometimes it's okay not to speak up—but this wasn't one of those times. A restaurant employee's role isn't just to take and process orders, but also to ensure, to the best of his or her ability, that the food they serve won't make customers sick. Through her poor personal hygiene, your manager was jeopardizing the health of patrons, and as much as you might like to feel otherwise, this is in fact your concern. Being reluctant to speak truth to power, as it were, is understandable, but you could at least have notified the assistant manager or a senior employee about what you observed, and that person could then address the issue directly with the manager. It is unlikely that handling the matter respectfully would result in your being fired, since your manager's own boss would likely agree that the manager's behavior was wrong.

Consider this, too: If you don't take action somehow, isn't it possible that your manager will continue practicing poor personal hygiene at work? By speaking up, you'll be protecting current as well as future customers. As we saw in the cheating example earlier, when you observe someone doing something they shouldn't, you're forced to make a tough decision, even though you haven't done anything improper.

Life Principle #1, "Do No Harm," on occasion requires us to take action to prevent harm to others. This situation is one such occasion.

Good Neighbors:
Being Fair to Classmates, Business Owners, and People You Hardly Know

You've probably heard the Golden Rule: "Do unto others as you would have them do unto you." You may also be familiar with the saying "Love thy neighbor as thyself." Both of these ideas are just another way of expressing Life Principle #5, "Be Loving." But what does it really mean to love thy neighbor, and why is this so important?

IS IT RIGHT TO BUY A CHILD'S TICKET AT THE MOVIES JUST BECAUSE YOU CAN GET AWAY WITH IT?

Q I look younger than I am. Generally, I'm not happy about this, but there is one advantage I have: when I go to the movies, I can pass for a child. Where I live, most of the movies charge a child admission for anyone up to the age of twelve, but even where the cutoff is eleven, I can still get by. If I'm with my friends, it doesn't work, but when I go with my parents, it does. My dad says it would be wrong for him to ask for a child ticket, since that's a lie, but if the person at the ticket booth assumes I'm a child, then it's okay. My mom, though, doesn't like doing this because she says it sets a bad example for me. My dad's response is that we're not hurting anyone and we're not exactly rich. Besides, we use the money we save to buy popcorn and candy, so the movie theater is getting our money one way or another. What do you say?

What Do You Think?

- Anyone who looks like they're still eleven or twelve shouldn't have to pay adult prices at the movies.
- I wouldn't feel right about doing this, but I wouldn't argue with my dad, either.
- I'd tell my dad to ask for an adult ticket for me, even though it's more expensive than a child's ticket.

A: A movie theater chooses to offer discounts as a courtesy to families with children and to senior citizens. Whether a theater decides to make the cutoff for children eleven, twelve, or thirteen, it's a fair rule, and thus Life Principle #4 calls upon us to follow it. Of course, not every theater policy is fair. Until the 1960s, many theaters required African Americans to sit in the balcony, and some banned them entirely. That was an unfair policy and deserved not to be followed. There is nothing wrong with the pricing plan for kids and adults, however. A father who doesn't want to pay the adult rate for you (which these days really is a lot of money) can choose not to take his family to the movies.

By allowing the movie theater to believe that you're a child when by their standards you're not, your dad is essentially saying that it's okay to do whatever is necessary to get ahead in some way. This has troubling implications that go far beyond seeing a movie. For example, when you're applying to college and you're sure that the school you want to attend won't check every little detail in your application, is it all right to say that you were the president of the Spanish club when you were actually just a member? Suppose you're at a restaurant and the waiter accidentally forgets to charge you for an appetizer. Is it acceptable to keep the error to yourself? When you're earning a living and some of your income is cash that the IRS wouldn't find out about, is it right not to declare that cash on your income tax? The answer to all three questions is no. It's wrong to deceive people or to act dishonestly.

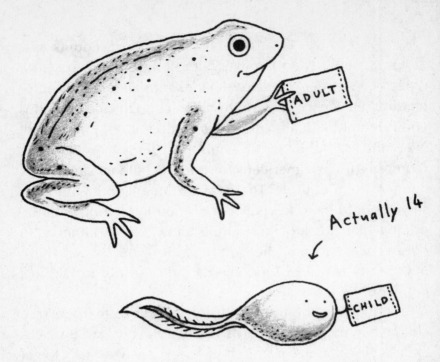

Actually 14

Looking young isn't the same as being young.

Third, the fact that you're spending the "extra" money at the concession stand doesn't justify being dishonest at the ticket booth. Doing the right thing isn't like doing math, where positive six cancels negative six in a sum. If something is wrong, it's wrong, and if it's unfair, it's unfair. Deceiving someone is a form of lying to them and is thus a violation of Life Principle #3, "Respect Others." Lying is an affront not just to others, but to ourselves as well, since we wind up damaging our own credibility and integrity.

In the long run, you're better off when you do the right thing rather than cutting corners to save a few dollars.

JUST BECAUSE YOU *CAN* DO SOMETHING DOES IT MEAN THAT YOU *SHOULD*?

Q: I found a great way to get new clothes: I buy them at a store that has a thirty-day return policy (no questions asked), I wear them a few times, and then I bring them back. I get a full refund and the chance to wear the latest fashions without really paying any money. My friend Emily says it's wrong for me to do this, because it's dishonest. I don't think it is at all, because I'm following the store's own policy. If you ask me, she's just jealous because she doesn't have the guts to do what I'm doing. Anyway, this store is part of a large chain, so they can afford it.

What Do You Think?

- If the store says it's okay, then it's okay.
- I wouldn't feel right about this somehow, even though technically the store does allow you to do this.
- Boo-hoo. I'm all choked up about how a multi-million dollar business is going to be out a few bucks for some clothes it won't be able to resell.

A: Emily is right. You're taking advantage of the store's return policy, and that is a straightforward violation of Life Principle #4, which calls upon us to give to others their due. The policy was created to give customers the freedom to buy clothes without having to worry that an ill-fitting sweater or blouse cannot be returned. Why would a company allow its customers to do what you're doing? A store is a business, not a public charity. If everyone behaved as you did, how long do you suppose the store could stay in business? Not for very long. Shouldn't the rules that apply to everyone else apply to you as well?

It's one thing to buy an outfit in good faith, take it home, realize that it's not right for you after all, and then return it for a refund or store credit. It's another to purchase something with the knowledge that you're going to wear it and then give it back. This betrays the trust that the store has placed in you to deal honestly with it and thus violates Life Principle #3, "Respect Others."

Now let's take a look at your statement that "this store is part of a large chain, so they can afford it." What does the size of a business have to do with how you deal with it? When you go to one of those so-called big-box stores and you see row after row of cosmetics, is it okay to steal a small tube of lip gloss just because "they can afford it"? Of course not. By the same token, buying a shirt you plan to wear and return is wrong, because you may be preventing the store from making

a profit on that shirt. Some stores won't resell clothes that have been returned, for good reason. Would you want to pay full price for a shirt you knew someone else had worn?

You've probably heard the term *business ethics*, which generally refers to how businesses should treat customers. The ethical business is one that offers a fair price for what it sells, provides good customer service, and doesn't make false claims about its products. But business ethics isn't just about what businesses owe customers. It's also about what customers owe businesses. We expect businesses to be fair to us. They have a right to expect us to be fair to them, too. This applies whether the business in question sells clothes, camcorders, video games, books—whatever.

I respectfully take issue with your statement that Emily lacks the guts to do what you're doing. It's not courageous to take advantage of a business, especially one that is trying to do right by its customers.

The situation raises an important question: Just because you *can* do something, does it mean that you *should* do it? The answer, as you can see here, is no.

GOING TO SCHOOL WHEN YOU'RE SICK ISN'T ANY FUN, BUT WHERE'S THE HARM?

Q: Last week one of my classmates came to school with a bad cold. It was disgusting; he was sneezing and coughing all day long. I didn't want to get his cold, so I said to him, "Why don't you stay home when you're sick?"

He replied, "Why don't you mind your own business?" Then he coughed right on me and laughed! Don't you think I was justified to say what I did? I don't think it's fair for someone to come to school with a cold and make everyone else sick.

What Do You Think?

• People can't help being sick. Just don't go near them!

• This guy was wrong. But it's not someone else's place to call him on it.

• If someone is doing something they shouldn't, whether in words or actions, they should be told. Otherwise, they'll never change.

A: Both of you could stand to come up with better ways of dealing with the things that bother you. It was obnoxious for your classmate to respond the way he did, since he could have given you his cold. At the same time, can you see how your question antagonized him?

Life Principle #5 calls upon us to treat others with kindness and compassion. The way you phrased your question could have been interpreted as a personal criticism, rather than as an expression of your concern for the both of you. It's understandable that you would want to protect yourself from getting another person's cold, but at the same time, it is a good thing to sympathize with someone who isn't feeling well. If your goal was to persuade him not to come to school sick, you could have said, "Hey, I'm sorry you're not feeling well. Wouldn't you rather stay home and take it easy? I'll take good notes for you, so you won't miss anything." If you were the sick one, wouldn't you prefer that approach to the one you used?

As far as the issue of coming to school with a cold or the flu is concerned, you're right: It's wrong. A sick person can pass germs to others through direct physical contact or simply by touching an object that another person then touches, like a door handle, computer keyboard, or pen. You can't give someone diabetes, asthma, or high blood pressure by touching them, but you can give them your cold or flu. (And, of course, just because someone is sneezing and coughing doesn't mean that person is contagious. He or she could have bad allergies or something else that can't be transmitted to other people.)

Recall that Life Principle #4 says that we ought to treat others fairly. Applying that principle to this situation means that someone with a cold should stay home from school, since doing otherwise is unfair to everyone. It's unfair to the people at school—students, teachers, the principal, the janitor—to increase the likelihood that they'll get sick. It's also unfair to the person who is sick.

Life Principle #1 says that we ought to do no harm, and going to school with a cold or flu compromises this responsibility as well.

Life Principle #5, "Be Loving," also applies to the issue of coming to school sick. I know I've mentioned this before, but it bears repeating: Doing the right thing refers not only to how we treat other people. It also refers to how we treat ourselves. It's simply unkind to ourselves to trudge to school with a cold, since it will take us longer to get better than if we stayed home to sleep, drink lots of water, and watch a movie or TV.

Many kids feel that they can't afford to miss a day at school. They want a perfect attendance score, or they're afraid they'll have too much work to do when they return. They may believe they'll be letting their teachers down, or maybe they like to learn and are happiest doing just that. It's admirable to want to do one's best all the time, but the fact is that sometimes we get sick, and when this happens, we have to take care of ourselves.

I don't feel so good...

Staying home when you have a contagious illness is the right thing to do. You owe it to yourself to rest and get better, and you owe it to others to avoid giving them your cold or flu.

WHAT AM I OWED WHEN I DO THE RIGHT THING?

Q Late last week, I was walking home from school and saw a black leather wallet lying on the ground. No one else was around. When I looked inside, I found credit cards, pictures, a driver's license, and over $150 in cash. I thought about taking the money and leaving the wallet, but I knew I'd feel guilty if I did that, and of course my parents would wonder where the money came from. I went home, told my mom what had happened, and said that I would track the guy down. My mom said she was proud of me for "doing the right thing." (I just smiled and kept my original plan to myself.)

Well, it wasn't hard to find the guy, since I had his full name and address. He was really relieved to hear that I'd found his wallet and said he'd come over right away to get it. I figured he would give me a reward for finding his wallet and going through the trouble of returning it, but guess what? All he did was say, "Thank you, thank you so much," over and over again. I kept waiting for him to open the wallet and pull out a fifty (or at least a twenty), but it never happened. A few days later, I got a thank-you note telling me how grateful he was and what a fine person I am for what I did.

Can you believe that? Doesn't he owe me at least a gift, if not cash? If it hadn't been for me, he never would have gotten his wallet back in the first place. He obviously could afford it, since he had so much money in the wallet. Also, a lot of people in my position would have just taken the money and left the wallet where it was (or maybe even used the credit cards). The whole thing makes me never want to "do the right thing" again.

What Do You Think?

- This guy was cheap not to give a reward for finding the wallet.
- Doing a good deed doesn't require any payback.
- If it happened to me, I'd come right out and ask, "Are you offering a reward?" before I gave him his wallet back.

A: Returning this gentleman's wallet was the right thing to do. However, if you did it only in hopes of getting a reward, I can see why you'd be disappointed.

Had the man posted flyers in the area saying "Reward for Return of Lost Wallet," then he would have had an obligation to give you some money, since the offer on the flyer is essentially a promise, and, as Life Principle #3 tells us, keeping our promises is an important way we show respect for other people. In lieu of such a promise, though, he had no obligation to pay you anything, and you had no right to expect anything

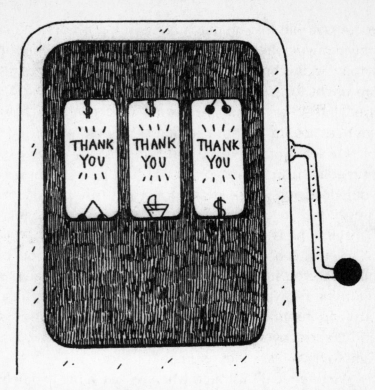

other than a thank-you. The only legitimate reason to do the right thing is simply because it is the right thing to do. If good things come of it, so much the better, but we err by feeling we're entitled to a reward for doing what is right.

Let's consider why this gentleman may have chosen not to give you money or buy you a gift. While it's true that he had $150 in his wallet, we can't conclude from this that he is wealthy. He may have just cashed his paycheck or gotten paid in cash for his labor, and this is all the money he has for an entire week. Some people pay their bills in cash, and this man might have been on his way to do just that. It's quite possible that he may not be in a position to give you any money without compromising his obligations to his family and/or himself. Life Principle #4, "Be Fair," says that we ought to give to others their due, and when resources are scarce, we must give priority to those who have the strongest claim to those resources. Wouldn't you be troubled to learn that he gave you some money at the expense of feeding his children or paying his bills? However noble your deed was, your desire for a reward should not take precedence over the needs of the man's family (or even himself, if he is single).

Even if the man turned out to be rich beyond belief, however, you still didn't have a right to expect to be paid for returning his wallet to him, because that wallet is his property and continues to be his property even while it is lost and then recovered. The only right at stake, really, was his right to have his wallet returned.

We often feel frustrated when we see a big gap between the way the world is and the way we think it ought be. One way to avoid unpleasant feelings in such situations is to know when there really is an "ought" in the first place. If you can put your disappointment aside, isn't it good to know that you helped another human being? You deserve to feel good about what you did.

Feeling good for having done the right thing is the best kind of reward there is, and it lasts far longer than whatever it was that you would have bought with the money you felt you were owed.

All About You:
Working Too Hard,
Dealing with Grief, and
Listening to Your Conscience

What should you do when you feel over-whelmed by anger? How should you handle the loss of someone close to you? Is it ever too late to right a wrong? It's just as troublesome to have no consideration for our own well-being as it is to be concerned only with it. This chapter looks at how you treat yourself, which is just as much an ethical issue as how you treat others.

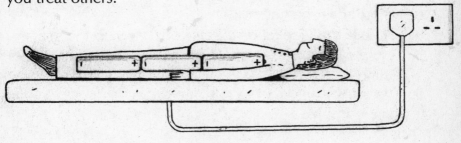

taking time to recharge

Q: I want to get into a good college, so I work really hard in school. In fact, everything in my life is geared toward achieving this goal. I'm in the honor society, I take music lessons, and I volunteer at the soup kitchen my church runs. This is on top of doing hours of homework every day. With all I have to do, I'm tired all the time. My diet isn't so hot, either, since I usually have only enough time to grab something and wolf it down fast. Believe me, I'd like to take it easy, but I'm afraid that if I do, then I won't get into the best college I can. My parents worked hard when they were teenagers, but from what they tell me, it wasn't as bad as it is now. What's the right way to handle all of this?

What Do You Think?

- Getting into the right college is the most important goal to focus on. Do whatever you have to do.
- Take it easy while you're young. It only gets harder as you get older.
- Use the weekends to relax but keep up the pressure during the week. You can't afford to fall behind.

A: You and your peers are facing tremendous pressure as you prepare for college and beyond. I commend you for being so diligent in doing all that you can to get into the school you want.

At the same time, you may be overdoing it. By being so focused on your goal that you're not able to eat well, sleep enough, or get exercise that refreshes and energizes you, you're not being fair to yourself. As Life Principle #4 reminds us, this is wrong in and of itself. But it also is self-defeating, because by working so hard that you're not at your best throughout the day, you won't be able to accomplish the very thing you're shooting for. How can you do well on a test if you can't keep your eyes open? If your stomach is growling, will you be at your best when you're taking a pop quiz in science? Taking care of yourself is both a kind thing to do and the best way for you to be successful in your quest.

Give yourself a break, literally and figuratively. Take a walk around the block from time to time. Watch one of your favorite TV shows. Take a nap. Do something that makes you laugh. Or just sit and do nothing. Treating yourself kindly in all that you do, especially when you're under duress, is a great way to apply Life Principle #5, "Be Loving." Whatever it takes to recharge your batteries and remain at your best is the right thing to do, the compassionate thing to do, and the surest way to achieve the goal you've set for yourself.

Q: My dad died a few months ago, and I feel overwhelmed with sadness. People who have lost a parent have told me that you never really "get over it," but that over time it gets easier to manage. I still find myself crying for no reason at all, and sometimes it's embarrassing (like when I'm in the middle of class or at a movie). Do the Life Principles have anything to say about losing someone close to me?

What Do You Think?

• Wow, if I lost one of my parents I would totally feel the same.
• It's okay to cry but not in class.
• So much crying might mean you need help to handle something so huge.

A: Having lost my own father not too long ago, this question has great personal resonance for me. Although my field is ethics, not psychology, I've come up with some guidelines for grief that are rooted in the five Life Principles and that may be helpful.

Recall that Life Principle #5, "Be Loving," means that we

should treat ourselves, and not just other people, in a kind and compassionate manner. Even if you're the sort of person who enjoys being social, now is the time to think of yourself, first and foremost. If this means retreating temporarily from the world, not answering the phone, and not chatting even with those in your innermost circle, there is nothing wrong with that. All you have to do is let others know in a polite way that you're not up to socializing. You can let them know that you appreciate any concern they have shown you. The rest is up to them.

Also, if ever there was a time to meet with a therapist or a trusted advisor from your faith, it is now. There is no shame in asking for help. In fact, just the opposite is true: No one can go it alone through one of the most traumatic experiences a person can have. Speaking at length with a caring professional is one of the best things you can do for yourself and is yet another way to apply Life Principle #5 to your own life.

It's true that you never get over the death of a parent (or, for that matter, any other family member or close friend). The lingering sadness is a way of honoring what that person still means to you. You can and should, however, find a way to manage the pain and to go on with your life. It may seem to be a violation of Life Principle #3, "Respect Others," to move on after losing someone close, but doing so is in fact a way to honor this principle. After all, the person you have lost would want that for you, just as you would want it for them.

You may find, as I did, that some of your friends will say or do things that strike you as cold, callous, or insensitive. You may get an e-mail of condolences from someone you wished had picked up the phone or visited. You may want to talk about what you're going through with someone who, for whatever reason, can't deal with it. Now is the time to be gentle with those who express their sympathy in an awkward fashion. Keeping Life Principle #5 in mind is especially valuable when dealing with folks who mean well but whose actions may be hurtful to you.

It is true that a friend should put his or her own feelings aside and focus on your needs at the moment. It is equally true, however, that as their friend, you should appreciate how uncomfortable they are and not expect them to behave as you might. Again, it is your ability to be kind and compassionate that will help you to do this.

By the same token, this ordeal may reveal who your true friends are. The people who stand by you now are people you will value for a long, long time.

Is it too late to make things right?

Q Last weekend I was mowing the lawn for some friends of my parents, the Smiths. I'm ashamed to confess this, but I took some money from a jar Mr. Smith keeps in the garage. The jar had lots of change and dollar bills, and I took only a few dollars and some change, so I'm sure they won't even notice.

The thing is, I've been feeling guilty all week long. I'm not even sure why I did it, since I knew I'd get paid for the job. I guess I just wanted to see if I could get away with it, which I did at first. But I keep thinking about what I did, and it's sometimes hard to concentrate at school. I'm not even sleeping well. In a way, it's not really a big deal. I mean, we're talking about less than ten bucks here. The thing is, I know that if I told my parents what I did, they'd make me give the money back to the Smiths, and I'm sure that the Smiths would never hire me again. If I tell the Smiths first, they'll call my parents, and I'll get in trouble. It feels like there's no way out, since keeping it to myself isn't working, either.

How do I get out of the situation I'm in? Isn't it too late to do anything about it, since it happened a week ago?

What Do You Think?

- Put it behind you and don't do anything like it again.
- Tell someone you trust so you can get it off your chest.
- Tell the Smiths and repay the money, then offer to mow their lawn for free. Once you make it right with them, you'll have a clear conscience.

A: It takes courage to admit that you did something wrong. A lot of people in this situation would just try to forget about it and find a way to rationalize what they had done. Some people wouldn't even be bothered by it the way you are. The fact that you feel guilty about your actions

It takes courage to lighten the load.

is a good thing: It means you have a conscience, and that it is in good shape.

If what you did is indeed not a big deal, why do you suppose you feel guilty at all? It's because you know in your heart that it's wrong to take something that doesn't belong to you. It doesn't matter if it's $10 or $10,000; it's still wrong. (Of course, if it had been the latter you'd taken, you'd have more than your conscience to worry about; you'd be worrying about getting arrested and being charged with a felony.)

Even if the Smiths never find out about what you did, stealing is stealing. Your action violates Life Principle #1, "Do No Harm." It also violates Life Principle #3, "Respect Others," since theft shows a great lack of respect for another person's property. Also, this principle calls upon us to be truthful. By pretending that nothing was wrong when the Smiths came home, you were essentially lying to them. Recall also that one aspect of Life Principle #4, "Be Fair," is the obligation to turn an unjust situation into a just one—or in other words, to right a wrong. The situation you're in now presents a challenge to do just that and thereby honor Life Principle #2, "Make Things Better," as well.

Now that we know what's going on ethically, let's consider some possible solutions. Returning the money to the Smiths and confessing what you've done won't necessarily mean that they'll never hire you again. That might turn out to be the case (and if it is, can you blame them?). However, it's also conceivable that the Smiths would be impressed by your courage in admitting that you did something you shouldn't have and the integrity to try to make things right again.

You, however, would do well to inform your parents about what has happened and what you intend to do now. In doing so, you will show your parents that not only do you know the difference between right and wrong, you're also willing to admit you made a mistake and accept the consequences for it.

It is never too late to right a wrong. Should you be willing to do this, you'll make things better for all concerned, including yourself. With a clear conscience, you will probably experience less anxiety during the day and find it much easier to sleep at night.

Is It Still Cheating If I Don't Get Caught?

You'd think that in a book whose title is the question "Is It Still Cheating If I Don't Get Caught?" you would be able to find an answer somewhere in the book. Well, you can find the answer, but it will have to come from you.

I invite you to use what you've learned in this book, and in all the experiences you've had in your life so far, to answer this question for yourself. Talk about it with your friends. Ask your parents what they think. If you're a person of faith, find out what your priest, minister, rabbi, or imam believes about it. But ultimately, you have to decide for yourself what the right answer is and to provide a solid argument for it. Which Life Principles are implicated by the question? If you believe that you're *not* cheating if you don't get caught, what might the consequences for yourself and others be if you are indeed able to get away with, say, copying another student's answers on a test or buying an essay for class on the Internet? What would the world be like if everyone believed as you do? If you believe, however, that cheating is cheating, no matter whether you're caught or not, how would you respond if other kids say something like, "Everybody cheats" or "You're a hypocrite, because I'm sure you've cheated at least once in your life"?

You now have the tools and skills to think carefully about questions like the one posed by the title of this book. Only you can decide how to apply these tools in your daily life, and only you can decide whether or not it's worthwhile to do so in the first place. Even when you know what you should do, it may take a great deal of courage to do it—and only you can find that courage. No one can do it for you.

You'll always be faced with tough decisions, but I hope that now you'll feel more confident about how to respond. May the five Life Principles serve as a GPS for the rest of your journey through this wonderful life.

HOW TO GET
A GOOD NIGHT'S SLEEP

At the end of every day, ask yourself:

- Did I avoid causing harm?
- Did I make things better in some way?
- Did I show respect to others?
- Was I fair?
- Was I loving?

If you can answer yes to all of these questions, you will be able to get a good night's sleep. You'll also have many reasons—five in particular—to be proud of yourself.

I know you can do it.

If you can't answer yes to all five questions, there's always tomorrow, and the night after that, and the night after that!

You have my permission to copy this page and put it next to your bed.

Acknowledgments

For the idea of presenting ethics in terms of five basic principles, I am indebted to a masterwork called *Principles of Biomedical Ethics* by Tom L. Beauchamp and James F. Childress. Published in its many editions by Oxford University Press, the book frames the ethical issues faced by healthcare providers and biomedical scientists in terms of what Beauchamp and Childress call the principles of nonmaleficence, beneficence, respect for autonomy, and justice. As I hope I've shown here, these principles apply to all of us. However, I've changed their names to make them accessible to a nonacademic audience. Thus, the principle of nonmaleficence becomes "Do No Harm," the principle of beneficence becomes "Make Things Better," the principle of respect for autonomy becomes "Respect Others," and the principle of justice becomes "Be Fair." To Beauchamp and Childress's quartet of principles, I have added a fifth, "Be Loving." One can locate this principle in the virtue of caring that Beauchamp and Childress discuss in their book, or in the works of the Reverend Dr. Martin Luther King, Jr., Mahatma Gandhi, and Mother Teresa, or, as Jeffrey Moses shows in *Oneness* (New York: Ballantine Books, 2002), in every great religious tradition the world has ever known. In short, I didn't come up with the five Life Principles; I'm merely distilling the lessons I've learned from the best among us.

I also wish to thank Kristen Bancroft, June Clark, Dr. T. Kaori Kitao, Deirdre Langeland, Patricia O'Connell, Peter Rubie, Dr. Robert Timko, and Lauren Wohl for their expert advice and generous support during the creation of this book. To Deborah Brodie, who initiated this project, I owe a special debt of gratitude. Students at Jesuit High School in Portland, Oregon, let me know about some of the ethical questions they find especially challenging, so to those students and the school's librarian, Mr. Gregory Lum, I offer a heartfelt thank-you.

I've been blessed by having had many superb teachers over the years, but one in particular deserves mention here. His name is Rand Dyer, and he became my fifth-grade teacher when my family and I moved from Baltimore to San Antonio in 1970. Until that time, I was an unruly child, to put it mildly. Mr. Dyer turned me around with a unique combination of wit, compassion, and discipline. I vividly remember this lecture to the class:

> If anyone ever offers you drugs, don't you dare take them. Ever. If you do, I'm going to haunt you. I will haunt you every day for the rest of your life.

This sounds like a threat when you just look at the words on a page, but at the time, I knew he was telling us this because he truly cared about us, and he wanted to protect us from the pernicious threat of drugs. Mr. Dyer loved each and every one of his students, and I can only hope to have some of the influence on young people today that he had on my classmates and me forty years ago.

Finally, there are two important people who, more than anyone else, helped me figure out the answers to life's tricky questions: my beloved parents, George and Sheila Weinstein. I love you, Mom. I miss you every day, Dad.

ASK THE ETHICS GUY . . . YOURSELF!

Do you have a question you'd like The Ethics Guy® to answer? Send it to ask@theethicsguy.com. Your question and his response may appear in a newspaper column, magazine article, or sequel to this book.

Send your answers to the question "Is it still cheating if I don't get caught?" to essay@theethicsguy.com, or visit TheEthicsGuy.com.

Index of Dilemmas

JUN 23 '09